From Fiction to Psychoanalysis

How can reading literary fiction shed light on the way we speak ourselves within psychoanalysis? Rather than offering psychoanalytic insights into literature, Rosemary Rizq, a practising psychologist and psychoanalytic psychotherapist, explores what literary fiction can bring to psychoanalysis.

In this fascinating collection of essays, she draws on stories written by authors ranging from Henry James to Kazuo Ishiguro and Colm Tóibín. By investigating the possibilities for 'fruitful encounter and dynamic exchange' between psychoanalysis and literature, Rizq sets out to offer a fresh perspective on theoretical ideas that are often presented within the psychoanalytic literature in abstract, overly technical ways. In a remarkably fresh approach, this book explores how fiction can inform, illuminate and even transform our understanding of psychoanalysis.

Written for practising clinicians, academics and students as well as for the wider public, this book offers an original and revealing perspective on the overlapping knowledge-claims and concerns of both literary fiction and psychoanalysis.

Rosemary Rizq is a psychologist chartered with the British Psychological Society, an HCPC-registered counselling psychologist and a UKCP-accredited psychoanalytic psychotherapist. She has worked extensively in the NHS as a psychologist and psychotherapist, authoring numerous papers on organizational dynamics as well as on psychotherapeutic training and clinical practice. She is currently professor of Psychoanalytic Psychotherapy at the University of Roehampton, with a part-time private practice in West London. She is co-editor of *The Industrialisation of Care*, published by PCCS Books in 2019.

This deeply-informed book is a brilliant exploration of the interrelations between the experience of literature and the concepts and practices of psychoanalysis. Since the 1970s both literary critics and psychoanalysts have increasingly recognized the inadequacy of "applied psychoanalysis" to capture and illuminate the fruitful possibilities of dialogue between these ways of knowing human subjectivity. Rosemary Rizq avoids the pull of master-narratives and hierarchic insistence on fixed truths and instead provides eloquent testimony to the value of reading in the potential spaces of both fields.

Murray Schwartz, *professor emeritus at Emerson College, Boston, Massachusetts, USA*

Rosemary Rizq's book is an amazingly lucid exposition of the common ground occupied by two eminently creative discourses: psychoanalysis and literature. It is rare to find an author equally at home in both these fields and Rizq provides us with a feast of riveting offerings. She accomplishes the almost impossible task of holding the tension between the enigmatic messages conveyed by literary giants such as Ishiguro, James and Toibin and identifying their traces and possible translations in the field of psychoanalytic theory and practice.

Anastasios Gaitanidis, *director, Relational Psychotherapy Ltd., and co-editor of* The Sublime in Everyday Life: Psychoanalytic and Aesthetic Perspectives, *Routledge (2020).*

Does one get a better understanding of people through studying psychology or literature? This book provides a too-rare antidote to the crisis in the psychological therapies by reconsidering literature with the help of psychoanalysis and 'ways of reading and telling'.

Del Loewenthal, *professor emeritus of Psychotherapy and Counselling, University of Roehampton, UK*

From Fiction to Psychoanalysis

Reimagining a Relationship

Rosemary Rizq

LONDON AND NEW YORK

Cover image: "Girl reading on a sofa" (1920), Isaac Israels (1880–1934); courtesy of Wikipedia Commons

First published 2023
by Routledge
4 Park Square, Milton Park, Abingdon, Oxon OX14 4RN

and by Routledge
605 Third Avenue, New York, NY 10158

Routledge is an imprint of the Taylor & Francis Group, an informa business

© 2023 Rosemary Rizq

The right of Rosemary Rizq to be identified as author of this work has been asserted in accordance with sections 77 and 78 of the Copyright, Designs and Patents Act 1988.

All rights reserved. No part of this book may be reprinted or reproduced or utilised in any form or by any electronic, mechanical, or other means, now known or hereafter invented, including photocopying and recording, or in any information storage or retrieval system, without permission in writing from the publishers.

Trademark notice: Product or corporate names may be trademarks or registered trademarks, and are used only for identification and explanation without intent to infringe.

Every effort has been made to contact copyright-holders. Please advise the publisher of any errors or omissions, and these will be corrected in subsequent editions.

British Library Cataloguing-in-Publication Data
A catalogue record for this book is available from the British Library

Library of Congress Cataloging-in-Publication Data
A catalog record has been requested for this book

ISBN: 978-1-032-35133-9 (hbk)
ISBN: 978-1-032-35134-6 (pbk)
ISBN: 978-1-003-32546-8 (ebk)

DOI: 10.4324/9781003325468

Typeset in Garamond
by Taylor & Francis Books

For Ali, who made it possible

Contents

Foreword		x
Acknowledgements		xiii
	Introduction: What do we know?	1
1	Copying, cloning and creativity: Kazuo Ishiguro's *Never Let Me Go*	21
2	The wager of faith in fiction and psychoanalysis: Colm Tóibín's *The Testament of Mary*	38
3	Psychoanalysis and ways of reading: Henry James's *The Figure in the Carpet*	56
4	Epistemologies of the particular: Tessa Hadley's *An Abduction*	75
5	On food, faith and psychoanalysis: Isak Dinesen's *Babette's Feast*	92
6	'Familiar artifice': Alice Munro's *The Moons of Jupiter*	110
	Index	132

Foreword

Art or science? This question, so frequently addressed to psychoanalysis, has the virtue of getting us to think about just what kind of thinking psychoanalysts are supposed to do. The problem lies in the form of the question, specifically the 'or', which imposes just the kind of binary that psychoanalysis was surely born to put in question. The bald alternatives seem to lend themselves to the lowest caricatures: the white-coated lab technician monitoring the rise and fall of dopamine levels on a screen as the wired-up patient dutifully free associates; the oracle in flowing tie-dyed robes enjoining the patient to dance their truth.

Freud was at times susceptible to this kind of sterile opposition. His 1908 'Creative Writers and Daydreaming', for example, sets art's aim of pleasure against science's aspiration to truth. Where the characters and stories of the novelist are conjured from the weightless realm of his daydreams and fantasies, the scientist is consigned to the far more cumbersome and resistant region we call reality, which forces him to learn, test and wait. But at least as often, Freud hints at an unnerving affinity between psychoanalysis and art. Both begin at, and seek to adumbrate, the outer edges of human experience, those strange and secret regions of the self irreducible to factual information or standardised metrics. And this is where the 'or' of 'art or science' misleads and distorts.

As Rosemary Rizq points out in her introduction to this wonderfully vital and illuminating book, Freud was aware from the outset, to the point of anxious self-consciousness, of the affinity of his case studies to narrative art and their consequent lack of 'the serious stamp of science'. In the 1895 *Studies on Hysteria*, he insists in a tone at once apologetic and defiant that the resemblance is none of his doing, but a consequence of 'the nature of the subject'.

Psychoanalytic and literary receptivity require us to do justice to the singularity of the speaking or writing voice. The attempt, in the name of scientific exactitude, to subsume that singularity under some diagnostic formula or critical terminology, can only result in a loss of exactitude. Psychoanalysis is a science that resembles literature – there is no 'or' here – because the truth it seeks is concealed inside, and inseparable from, the baggy, digressive and contradictory forms of human speech.

From this perspective, and in spite of its graciously understated claims, Rizq's book is far more than a series of psychoanalytic essays on literature; it is a penetrating and original contribution to the vexed question of the relationship of psychoanalysis to its neighbouring disciplines. Rather than 'claim' psychoanalysis for art or literature, she shows how and why the forms of psychoanalytic knowledge are liable to become literary. Far from being a preference for a more impressionistic or partial form of knowledge, the literariness of psychoanalysis is the paradoxical sign and seal of its precision.

This may be why Rizq at various points writes herself discreetly and movingly into her readings, deftly weaving stories of her early musical education and first communion into her chapters on texts by Ishiguro and Dinesen. These passages aren't mere anecdotal illustrations, but ways of showing the ineliminable subjectivity that insinuates itself into the practice of psychoanalytic thinking and reading. They are instances of what she rather beautifully describes as 'a stubborn core of semantic incommensurability that resists any attempt at equivalence or substitution'.

Under her generous gaze, psychoanalytic and literary texts are exemplary hosts to that which resists 'equivalence or substitution', to an otherness beyond measure. Her choices of literary texts amplify this spirit of hospitality; while they are all very different, they converge on a concern with some element of the human that evades capture, ensuring the essential 'incompleteness' of every story we seek to tell about our lives.

This otherness is hardly the exclusive domain of psychoanalysis; hence Rizq's fascinating forays beyond psychoanalysis and into metaphysics and religion, giving her book an expansiveness that is never at the expense of its precise attention to textual detail.

In her conclusion to her immersive reading of James' great short story, 'The Figure in the Carpet', Rizq traces an affinity between James and Winnicott (who, I discover to my delight here, devoured James as a young man) in terms of a shared concern with 'hospitality to that which is strange or other within the text'. This is the very model of criticism she comes not only to describe but to model in this intricately linked series of essays.

It is common for writers working in the space between psychoanalysis and literature these days to insist on their resistance to diagnostic, psychobiographical or metapsychological reductionism. But few succeed in really drawing out the singularity of the literary text. Precisely because she takes up a stance of humility, renouncing any claim to have resolved its enigmas or revealed its secrets, Rizq is able to forge ways for us to read and (at least as importantly) take a specifically psychoanalytic pleasure in literature.

One of the aphorisms in *Windows*, a volume by the great French analyst J.-B. Pontalis, reads simply, 'Dreams, poetry, psychoanalysis: exact sciences'. If you wish to understand what he means, look no further than this fascinating and singularly generous book.

Josh Cohen, September 2021
Psychoanalyst in private practice and Professor of
Modern Literary Theory at Goldsmiths,
University of London

Acknowledgements

These essays have been written over a number of years and I owe much to my clinical and academic colleagues who, in different ways, have helped me to develop my ideas and have encouraged and supported me in my writing.

Rachel Darnley-Smith, Anastasios Gaitanidis and Edith Steffen at the University of Roehampton each read or heard some of these essays at different times and offered incisive comments and ideas, many of which have found their way into the final versions offered here. I am grateful in particular to Edith Steffen for a rich and illuminating discussion about grief and loss in Wordsworth's *We are Seven*, which inspired the introduction to this book. James Mann and Joanna Gardner from the Site for Contemporary Psychoanalysis, along with other colleagues there, warmly encouraged me to follow my interest in psychoanalysis and fiction. Tessa Hadley very generously offered a penetrating and inspiring commentary on a first draft of 'An Abduction' and I have been particularly fortunate to benefit from Ann Scott's long and exceptional editorship of the *British Journal of Psychotherapy*, where she and her outstanding reviewers offered engaged and thoughtful critiques of early versions of several of the papers presented here. Without the warm support of Murray Schwartz, Editor-in-Chief of *American Imago*, I am not sure the book would have got off the ground at all and I remain deeply grateful for his consistent and kind encouragement. I am also immensely grateful to the American Psychoanalytic Association for awarding me the Peter Loewenberg Essay Prize for the final essay in this book, 'Familiar Artifice', and for inviting me to present it at the American Psychoanalytic Association's National Conference in February 2021. A stimulating discussion there with Mitchell Wilson and other colleagues added enormously to the current version. Other friends and colleagues, many more than I am able to mention here, have also informed my thinking in richly helpful ways including: Russel Ayling, Nicky De Fries, Mark Donati, Jo Joyce, Birgit Kuypers, and Julie Walsh. My patients and my students at the University of Roehampton are, as ever, my best teachers; over the years, they have all consistently pushed, pressed and provoked me to find new ways of thinking about fiction and psychoanalysis. They have contributed more than I can say.

On the home front, my wonderfully patient husband, Johnny, my inspirational daughter, Victoria, and my son Michael – my best, most exacting interlocutor! – have all stood by, challenging and encouraging me with kindness, love and great forbearance right up until the moment I finally succeeded in putting this book to bed.

***

Several of the essays in this volume started off life as talks and have subsequently been published in different versions in various academic journals with permission to reproduce as follows:

'Copying, Cloning, and Creativity: Kazuo Ishiguro's *Never Let Me Go*' was first published in *British Journal of Psychotherapy* (2014), 30, 4: 517–532, here reprinted with permission, © John Wiley and Sons. A shorter version was given as a talk in January 2014 at the Site for Contemporary Psychoanalysis in London.

'The Wager of Faith in Literature and Psychoanalysis: Colm Tóibín's *The Testament of Mary*' was first published in *British Journal of Psychotherapy* (2019), 35, 4: 610–627, here reprinted with permission, © John Wiley and Sons.

'Psychoanalysis and Ways of Reading: Henry James' *The Figure in the Carpet*' first appeared in *American Imago* (2018), 75, 4: 517–542. Copyright © 2018 John Hopkins University Press.

'Epistemologies of the Particular: Tessa Hadley's *An Abduction*' is a considerably edited and revised version of a talk first given in 2020 for the Southern Association for Psychotherapy and Counselling in London. In addition, this article was formerly published in *Psychodynamic Practice* (2021), 28, 1: 8–24.

'On Food, Faith and Psychoanalysis: Isak Dinesen's *Babette's Feast*' was first published in *British Journal of Psychotherapy* (2017), 33, 4, 537–554, here reprinted with permission, © John Wiley and Sons. A rather different version was given and discussed at at a talk for the Research Centre for Therapeutic Education Group at the University of Roehampton.

"Familiar Artifice": Alice Munro's 'The Moons of Jupiter' is a revised and extended version of a paper presented and discussed at the National Meeting of the American Psychoanalytic Association in February 2021. It was subsequently published by the Journal of the American Psychoanalytic Association (2022), 70:1, 77–102.

***

The author also gratefully acknowledges permission to reprint excerpts from the following fictional texts:

Excerpt(s) from *The Moons of Jupiter* by Alice Munro published by Macmillan. Copyright © 1982 by Alice Munro. Reprinted by permission of William Morris Endeavor Entertainment, LLC on behalf of Alice Munro.

Excerpt(s) from *The Moons of Jupiter* by Alice Munro published by Vintage. Copyright © Alice Munro 1982. Reprinted by permission of The Random House Group Limited.

Excerpt(s) from *The Moons of Jupiter* by Alice Munro, copyright © 1977, 1978, 1979, 1980, 1981, 1982 by Alice Munro. Used by permission of Alfred A. Knopf, an imprint of the Knopf Doubleday Publishing Group, a division of Penguin Random House LLC. All rights reserved.

Excerpt(s) from *Bad Dreams and Other Stories* by Tessa Hadley published by Jonathan Cape. Copyright © Tessa Hadley 2017. Reprinted by permission of The Random House Group Limited.

Excerpt(s) from *The Testament of Mary* by Colm Tóibín published by Penguin. Copyright © The Heather Blazing Ltd, 2012. Reprinted by permission of Penguin Books Limited.

Excerpt(s) from *The Testament of Mary* by Colm Tóibín. Copyright © 2012 Colm Tóibín. Reprinted by permission of McClelland & Stewart, a division of Penguin Random House Canada Limited. All rights reserved.

Excerpt(s) from *Never Let Me Go* by Kazuo Ishiguro, Copyright © 2005 Kazuo Ishiguro. Reprinted by permission of Alfred A. Knopf Canada, a division of Penguin Random House Canada Limited. All rights reserved.

Excerpt(s) from *Never Let Me Go* by Kazuo Ishiguro. Copyright © 2005 by Kazuo Ishiguro. Used by permission of Alfred A. Knopf, an imprint of the Knopf Doubleday Publishing Group, a division of Penguin Random House LLC. All rights reserved.

Excerpt(s) from *Never Let Me Go* by Kazuo Ishiguro, Copyright © 2005 Kazuo Ishiguro. Reprinted by permission of Faber and Faber Ltd.

Introduction
What do we know?

In what is often described as one of his 'minor' papers, Freud (1910) tells the story of how he was consulted by a middle-aged, divorced woman who came to him complaining of anxiety. She had previously consulted a young, local doctor who advised her, based on what was clearly a rather limited understanding of a new psychoanalytic form of treatment, that her anxiety was probably the result of sexual frustration. Various practical suggestions about how she could remedy this dismaying condition ensued, but none of them seemed to be acceptable to her. No doubt irritated by her refusal to accept his recommendations, the young doctor referred her to Freud who, as the one responsible for this 'new discovery' (p. 351) of psychoanalysis, was presumably expected to confirm the accuracy of his diagnosis.

Perhaps it is not surprising that an apparently minor paper of Freud's should turn out to conceal something more significant. For just as marginal elements within a dream turn out to be particularly telling indices of the patient's unconscious desire, so too a rather ordinary clinical case is used by Freud to smuggle in a cautionary tale that illustrates the kind of knowledge he thinks is appropriate to psychoanalytic work. 'It is a long superseded idea', he writes,

> and one derived from superficial appearances, that the patient suffers from a sort of ignorance, and that if one removes this ignorance by giving him information (about the causal connection of his illness with his life, about his experiences in childhood, and so on) he is bound to recover. The pathological factor is not his ignorance in itself, but the root of this ignorance in his inner resistances; it was they that first called this ignorance into being, and they still maintain it now. The task of the treatment lies in combating these resistances ... If knowledge about the unconscious were as important for the patient as people inexperienced in psycho-analysis imagine, listening to lectures or reading books would be enough to cure him. Such measures, however, have as much influence on the symptoms of nervous illness as a distribution of menu-cards in a time of famine has upon hunger.
>
> (p. 354)

Offering 'information', suggests Freud, not only demonstrates poor understanding of psychoanalytic theory; it is poor technique. The issue is not simply that the patient doesn't know something, but rather that she resists knowing it. Indeed, her suffering is not so much a consequence of, but rather is itself constituted by resistance and the resulting ignorance cannot be remedied simply by informing her about the workings of her unconscious. The comparison of information with menu cards in a time of famine suggests that substituting instruction for lack of awareness is not only futile, but cruel; and despite Freud's professional politesse, the maladroit young doctor seems to come in for some rather heavy, if implicit, criticism. But what interests Freud here is not simply that a little knowledge is a dangerous thing; it is the way resistance itself seems to point to a particular kind of knowing, as if the patient's very unknowing announces an altogether different epistemology at work behind the scenes. The patient's words testify to a form of knowing that is neither available to its speaker nor amenable to any alternative intellectual enlightenment. The young doctor's crude attempts to know the patient better than she knows herself only serve to strengthen her determination to remain ignorant. Unconscious knowing thus appears to be of a different order, perhaps even inimical, to the kind of knowing that Freud thinks is acquired through receiving 'information' or 'listening to lectures'.

I have always been curious about this kind of knowing: the kind that resists our formal systems of knowledge and their traditional epistemologies. As a psychologist and psychoanalyst, it has often seemed to me that our contemporary valorisation of academic, scientific and theoretical forms of knowing has come at the expense of understanding and celebrating the subtle, elusive and sometimes inarticulate forms of knowing that emerge in the everyday cut and thrust of psychotherapeutic work. Of course, we need to remember from the outset that the terms 'knowing' and 'knowledge' are deeply contentious and very far from neutral. They are terms that may be said to have value, often implying something rather concrete like a lump of coal that we can dig out of the ground, as if knowledge is something to be sought and found, acquired, overlooked or even something that can go missing. But knowledge is not to be found in the same way as a lump of coal is to be found. While there is generally little dispute about what constitutes coal, there is significant disagreement about what constitutes knowledge. Any claim to knowledge in the world these days is likely to meet with a degree of scepticism if not outright distrust; our sources of information are subjected to intense scrutiny and empirical evidence is required to back up our assertions. Our notion of knowledge, indeed the entire history of knowledge, is imbued with ideas of claim and counter-claim, of argument, debate and disagreement. In psychoanalysis and in the psychotherapeutic field more widely, what we are able to 'know' of the patient and the nature of the psychological knowledge we accrue in clinical work has always been a matter of fierce epistemological dispute.

This issue becomes even more complicated when we ask what is meant by 'psychological' knowledge. Psychology is a somewhat confusing term that has connotations straddling both the scientific and the artistic worlds. There is the kind of psychology that happens in science and there is the kind of psychology that happens in art, particularly literary fiction, and it is important here to try to distinguish between the two. By and large, the kind of psychology that happens in science is the kind that is concerned with predicting what people do and how they behave in particular circumstances and contexts. In the clinical field, it is commonly concerned with classifying, diagnosing and treating emotional problems according to general laws and principles. Anticipating this, Freud's (1896) intention in his early, unfinished 'Project for a Scientific Psychology' was to 'furnish a psychology that shall be a natural science: that is, to represent psychical processes by establishing quantitatively determinate states of specifiable material particles, thus rendering those processes perspicuous and free from contradiction' (p. 295). Yet only a year after Freud's 'Project', he was to lose interest in the question of how to represent the psychical apparatus in terms of neuro-physiology, and his attention was diverted towards understanding the unconscious basis of hysteria. Modern psychology, as we know, turned to behaviourism; but lately it has shown a tendency to revert to the ambitious trajectory originally set by Freud, drawing on neuroscience and genetics in an effort to establish scientific knowledge about the way the mind operates.

The kind of psychology that happens in literature, on the other hand, has no such ambitions. If '[l]iterature', as Roland Barthes (1977) remarks, 'accommodates many kinds of knowledge' (p. 6), the imaginative remit of literary fiction might be said to accommodate an entirely different kind of knowledge of the mind than the kind proposed by scientific psychology. Its responsibilities and interests are quite distinct from the obligations and concerns of science. When Virginia Woolf (1925) writes of Mrs Dalloway that 'she had a perpetual sense, as she watched the taxi cabs, of being out, out, far out to sea and alone; she always had the feeling that it was very, very dangerous to live even one day' (p. 6), we are immediately inside Mrs Dalloway's head; we are concerned with her interior world, with imagining what it might be like for her to go shopping, to feel in the midst of busyness the terror and anxiety of being all alone in the sea of life. What we might call literary psychology, then, is not primarily interested in identifying what is going on in our brains, nor is it concerned merely with conveying information about what we do or how we behave. Rather it is interested in what it is *like* to think, feel and act a certain way. It is concerned with the nature of experience or, to be more precise, with experience in the sense of living through something: with what Dorothy Walsh (1969) calls 'imaginative participation' (p. 138). The capacity of literary fiction to engage the reader in an act of 'imaginative participation' may be one of the reasons that Freud was to remain somewhat ambivalent about exactly which kind of psychology he was really interested in. Anxious to establish the scientific credentials of his new psychoanalytic treatment, he was nonetheless profoundly influenced by art, literature and myth and thought they could bring something particularly valuable to psychoanalytic work. In 1896, the very same year as his 'Project', he admitted that:

> local diagnosis and electrical reactions lead nowhere in the study of hysteria, whereas a detailed description of mental processes such as we are accustomed to find in the works of imaginative writers enables me, with the use of a few psychological formulas, to obtain at least some kind of insight into the course of that affliction.
>
> (p. 165)

Imaginative writers, for Freud, bring to psychoanalytic work a kind of understanding, a particular kind of 'knowing', which scientific or theoretical writing might be seen to lack.

How can we characterise this literary kind of knowing? And how can we how think about its relationship to the peculiar kind of knowing that we call psychoanalytic? If psychoanalysis has always been thought of as a rather 'knowing' kind of discipline, one that harbours the secrets of the unconscious, can we think of a work of fiction as harbouring a secret knowledge of its own? If it is one thing to be curious about what the patient comes to know during the course of a psychoanalysis, it is quite another, I think, to be curious about what a novel or a short story might be supposed to know. Does it even make sense to think of literature as 'knowing' anything at all? Can we allow ourselves to think of a text as 'knowing' or even 'resisting' in a way that is analogous to the way a patient might know something, or resist knowing, in analytic treatment? Perhaps we do not need not go into the entire history of philosophy here to remember that the knowledge-claims of literature have been a bone of contention for a long time. They go back at least as far as Plato's scepticism towards poetry and his decision to banish poets from the *Republic*. Recently, however, there has been renewed interest from a number of writers (see e.g. de Bolla, 2001; Gourgouris, 2003; Macherey, 1990; Wood, 2005) in defending the idea that literature can 'know' something, that it constitutes a specific mode of knowledge that is different from knowledge-claims requiring empirical verification. 'What literature knows', writes Michael Wood (2005),

> what a novel or poem or play knows, is strictly, unfiguratively, what I now know that I didn't know before I read the text; or what I only half-knew before; and perhaps even now cannot articulate as knowledge. And while this may be less than the author knew – and often is, alas – it may also be more, or different.
>
> (p. 112)

I find this a useful statement to be going on with, not the least because it draws attention to the way in which a work of literary fiction might possess a certain unsettling element of its own, a kind of knowledge within and of itself that lies beyond authorial intention and to which it alone, rather than anyone else, is party. It is the kind of knowledge, Wood hints, that cannot be possessed or intellectually grasped though it may, albeit partially, be sensed or experienced.

Of course, a text is not a person. Like Derek Attridge (2009), I am charmed and troubled in equal measure about the implied anthropomorphism in the notion that a novel or a poem might itself be able to 'know' something rather merely being a vehicle through which to express, inspire or deliver a certain kind of knowledge. But Wood's statement allows me to put personification to work as a device, a kind of rhetorical strategy that enables me to bridge the kind of 'knowing' that he claims for literature with the kind of 'knowing' we might think of as characteristic of psychoanalysis. For Wood's ideas vividly parallel the way the patient in analysis unconsciously knows something that the analyst does not; and how, during the course of therapy, the analyst may come to learn something from his or her patient that he 'didn't know before', or 'only half-knew'; and which even after working with the patient for some time, he or she may not be able consciously to comprehend or 'articulate as knowledge'. And while this partial, provisional kind of analytic 'knowing' will certainly be different from the patient's kind of 'knowing', the aim of psychoanalysis is to become aware of and pursue whatever can be gleaned from that unsettling domain of unconscious knowledge that may only fleetingly be glimpsed or tacitly sensed rather than firmly possessed or intellectually mastered.

The idea that literature and psychoanalysis might share an interest in these kinds of knowledge-claims, that reading a work of fiction might tell us something about the (rather different) notion of 'reading' the patient in psychoanalysis, is what lies behind this book's attempt to bring both these disciplines into closer dialogue. I recognise, however, that some of my colleagues in the psychoanalytic field may view this attempt with some dismay. These days, any suggestion that psychoanalysis might align itself more closely to the interpretative disciplines of the arts and the humanities than to a scientifically-validated form of psychological treatment risks resurrecting heated historical debates and long-standing interdisciplinary stand-offs. Indeed, the relationship between psychoanalysis and literature turns out to be one more akin to an uneasy truce between battle-scarred sparring partners than an affiliation between like-minded soulmates. Whilst Freud himself anticipated an alliance between psychoanalysis and literary studies – a union heralded by his 1908 essay *Creative Writers and Daydreaming* – it was his own remarkable literary abilities that were to set in motion an enduring but fertile tension between the scientific, empirical rationale for the psychoanalytic project on the one hand, and its creative, imaginative appeal on the other. As Kazin (1961) argues, it was Freud's use of language 'as supple, dramatic and charged with the excitement of Freud's mission as a "conquistador" into realms hitherto closed to scientific inquiry, that excited and persuaded so many readers of his books' (pp. 382–3). Famously, it did not persuade the psychologist Hans Eysenck (1985), who roundly dismissed Freud as 'a genius, not of science, but of propaganda, not of rigorous proof, but of persuasion, not of the design of experiments, but of literary art. His place is not, as he claimed, with Copernicus and Darwin, but with Hans Christian Andersen and the Brothers Grimm, tellers of fairy tales' (p. 208). Others will see any attempt to bring psychoanalysis and fiction closer together as indexing a return to seemingly fruitless debates about the division between the natural and the human sciences and where the field of psychoanalysis may best be located (for discussions see e.g. Grunbaum, 1984; Habermas, 1971; Hoffman, 2009; Ricoeur, 1970; Wallerstein, 2009).

Literary critics too have their suspicions about deploying theoretical models from another discipline within their own field of expertise. Although psychoanalysis has very successfully been imported as a critical tool in the analysis of literary texts, orthodox Freudian psychoanalytic readings that traditionally seek to 'explain' their unconscious meaning or that delve into the unconscious motives of authors and their fictive characters raise considerable doubts about the value of such an exercise. Felman (1977) has argued that the master-discourse of psychoanalysis too frequently claims an interpretative priority to which literature must slavishly yield. Despite subsequent Lacanian and Derridean forays into more subtle, post-structuralist critical readings, the propensity of psychoanalytic literary criticism to assume a hidden or repressed core of meaning and to close down rather than open up textual debate is one reason why Brooks (1987) has gone so far as to suggest that psychoanalytic literary criticism has always been 'something of an embarrassment' (p. 334).

Interesting and important as the above debates are, this is neither a book about the validity of psychoanalysis as a treatment nor is it a book of – or even about – psychoanalytic literary criticism. Indeed, as an amateur student of literature I am in no position to write one, even though as a psychoanalytic clinician I will claim the right to borrow from literary criticism where it suits my purposes. But my aim must be more modest. Rather than simply deploying psychoanalysis to promote a 'paranoid' reading of literary texts, as Eve Kosofsky Sedgwick (1997) would have it, I am more interested in finding out whether psychoanalysis and literature might have something useful to say to each other. Rather than reading suspiciously, then, I am more interested in reading suggestively; instead of imposing explanation and interpretation, I will be more attentive to sources of appreciation and inspiration, exploring how psychoanalysis and literature might be, as Adam Phillips (2002) recommends, 'complementary and not solely antagonistic' (p. 2). Both fields after all might be said to be concerned with the telling of stories: the patient's personal story that is elicited, developed and in some cases changed through the psychoanalytic process; and the writer's fictional tale that is developed via the use of his or her imagination. I have been particularly concerned with trying to reimagine and elucidate what I see as the nature of the relationship between these different kinds of storytelling and, more importantly, with demonstrating how their distinctive contributions might work together creatively and productively, as much by their shared commitments and concerns as by their ability to complicate each other in interesting ways. This collection of loosely-related essays does not attempt to provide a comprehensive overview of what might be thought of as a rather unwieldy and historically controversial interdisciplinary field; nor does it aim to further any grand debate about the putative 'correspondence', as Brooks (1987) once proposed, 'between literary and psychic processes' (p. 337). Rather, I have tried to place my readings of various works of fiction in some kind of dialogue with psychoanalysis in order to illuminate and extend the possibilities for fruitful encounter and dynamic exchange. Of course, anything that is written over a period of years will inevitably expose certain personal preferences and preoccupations. In retrospect, the stories and authors I have selected turn out to have been the ones that have got under my skin, so to speak; they are the ones that have most charmed, gripped and captivated me, usually for reasons that I did not fully understand at the time of reading. It has, in truth, been sobering to realise that the works of fiction I have chosen – and the psychoanalytic theories I draw on in this book – reveal less about my formal or conscious intentions and much more about what resonates with my previously inarticulate and perhaps unconscious interests, investments and affiliations. Some of the essays in this book are directly concerned with understanding and clarifying particular psychoanalytic concepts and ideas. For example, in 'Copying, Cloning and Creativity' (Chapter 1) and 'On Food, Faith and Psychoanalysis' (Chapter 5), I have explored issues of unconscious identification, musing on sources of selfhood and subjectivity through a reading of stories by Kazuo Ishiguro and Isak Dinesen. In others, I have been curious about the way fiction itself seems to illuminate something about psychoanalytic work. For example, in 'The Wager of Faith' (Chapter 2) and 'Psychoanalysis and Ways of Reading' (Chapter 3), I have drawn on Colm Tóibín and Henry James respectively to explore how the reading of a text offers a gateway to understanding the quality and reception of alterity within psychoanalysis. In 'Epistemologies of the Particular' (Chapter 4), my reading of a story by Tessa Hadley examines the relationship between the knowledge claims of fiction and those of the psychoanalytic case history; and in 'Familiar Artifice' (Chapter 6), a story by Alice Munro allows me to explore how the short story form provides a literary model for the kind of subjectivity that emerges in the telling of a self within psychoanalysis.

In each chapter of the book, I have juxtaposed my reading of a work of literary fiction with a variety of psychoanalytic ideas or texts drawn from theorists ranging from Freud and Winnicott to Laplanche and Kristeva. But rather than making my primary focus what psychoanalysis brings to an understanding of fiction, rather than privileging the presumed theoretical authority of psychoanalysis, I have positioned my reading of psychoanalytic texts at a somewhat different angle to my chosen works of fiction. Instead of moving from psychoanalysis to fiction, as is traditionally the case, I have wanted to move *from* fiction *to* psychoanalysis, exploring how a work of fiction itself might inform, illuminate, even transform our understanding of psychoanalysis. If, as Felski (2020) comments, 'we often give art an exceptional credit for ushering newness into the world' (p. 100), perhaps the art that is fiction can invigorate and re-animate how we approach, encounter and engage with psychoanalytic ideas and concepts. All too often, the demands of conventional academic inquiry mean these tend to be discussed and written about 'in ways that drain the life from them and transform them into technical jargon' (Ogden and Ogden, 2012, p. 244). As a practising clinician, too, I am aware that the theoretical frameworks underpinning our therapeutic work can sometimes seem overly dry and abstract. Sensitivity to complex issues of ethics and confidentiality means that the kind of detailed clinical examples through which we, like Freud, have traditionally been able to flesh out, illustrate and interrogate familiar ideas and theoretical constructs are now far less frequently published. So by turning to fiction, by bringing psychoanalysis into contact with other kinds of writing – other texts, other stories, other authors – my wager is that psychoanalysis might stand to gain something from her literary 'other'. Indeed, in this respect, I follow Frosh (2010) who points out that

> psychoanalysts who recommend the development of literary capacities as a way of mastering technique have something useful to say not only because of what there is to be learned from the practice of literature, but also because working reflexively in this way leaves psychoanalysis itself open to challenge and change.
>
> (p. 76)

In the spirit of 'challenge and change' then, and by way of introducing my methods to the reader, I will start with a reading of a poem that I think speaks to many of the above ideas: Wordsworth's *We Are Seven*. First published in the *Lyrical Ballads* of 1798, this is a poem that has received a number of persuasive critical interpretations, amongst which I have found de Bolla's (2001) discussion of knowledge in the poem particularly compelling. I will draw on de Bolla in my own analysis, but want to proceed by situating my response to the poem alongside a reading of Sandor Ferenczi's (1932) 'Confusion of the Tongues', a paper that is famously concerned with critiquing the kind of knowledge frequently claimed in traditional psychoanalytic interpretation. I will not attempt a comprehensive analysis of either text; my readings will inevitably be brief, partial and tentative. But along the way, I hope to reflect on some of the shared concerns and mutual interests of psychoanalysis and literature in a way that allows me to advance, if only incrementally and incompletely, towards my reimagined relationship between these two fields.

We Are Seven

In his 'Preface' to the 1802 edition of the *Lyrical Ballads*, Wordsworth claims his purpose was to

> choose incidents and situations from common life, and to relate or describe them throughout, as far as was possible, in a selection of language really used by men, and at the same time, to throw over them a certain colouring of imagination, whereby ordinary things should be presented to the mind in an unusual aspect.
>
> (p. 33)

One of the 'ordinary things' presented to the reader was his recollection of a visit to Goodrich Castle in 1793, where Wordsworth met a little girl who was to become the model for the child in the poem *We Are Seven*. In this sixteen-stanza ballad, a little 'cottage girl' is asked by a rather pedantic adult man how many siblings she has, and she tells him 'we are seven' whilst maintaining that two have died. The adult reckons five living children and two dead as five; the child herself obstinately reiterates that 'we are seven'. The dialogue shifts back and forth between the adult who insists on reasoning with the child, and the little girl who calmly asserts, in the face of her interlocutor's mounting irritation, that her two dead siblings should be counted amongst the tally of the living.

In his earlier 1800 'Preface', Wordsworth tells us that the poem was intended to demonstrate 'the perplexity and obscurity which in childhood attend our notion of death, or rather our utter inability to admit that notion' (p. 126). But we might want to acknowledge from the outset how the oddly unstable syntax of this explanatory sentence invites a variety of possible interpretations: that children are ignorant of death and that we too as adults are unable to admit to our mortality; that in comparison to the immature child's 'perplexity' 'our utter inability', as adults, to 'admit' the fact of death is all the greater; or even that, as adults, we are unable to 'admit' our inability to fathom how children themselves might conceive of death. Despite the fact that we were all children once, perhaps we have forgotten what it is that we once knew. As adults, we have become blind to the kind of knowledge entailed by a child's ignorance and we are oblivious to other forms of knowing that might lie hidden within the folds, the 'perplexity and obscurity', of childhood. Perhaps, to take this reading one step further, our own difficulty in imagining how children think and feel about death ensures that we ourselves remain unable to 'admit' its enormity and fundamental impenetrability. Indeed, if 'the Child is father of the Man' as Wordsworth (1802) goes on to write later, we might conclude that our inability to 'know' the child necessarily brings about a failure to 'know' ourselves as adults; and so the child's apparent ignorance of death merely serves to hold up a mirror to our own failures of self-knowledge.

Whichever reading we prefer, I suggest that Wordsworth at the very least conveys a certain curiosity about 'our utter inability to admit' something; and that from the outset the poem stages a scene of inquiry in which what it might mean to 'admit' a particular kind of knowledge appears to be at stake. The poem is as follows:

> A simple child, dear brother Jim,
> That lightly draws its breath,
> And feels its life in every limb,
> What should it know of death?
>
> I met a little cottage girl,
> She was eight years old, she said:
> Her hair was thick with many a curl
> That clustered round her head.
>
> She had a rustic woodland air,
> And she was wildly clad;
> Her eyes were fair, and very fair
> – Her beauty made me glad.
>
> "Sisters and brothers, little maid,
> How many may you be?"
> "How many? seven in all", she said,
> And wondering looked at me.
>
> "And where are they, I pray you tell?"
> She answered "Seven are we,
> And two of us at Conway dwell,
> And two are gone to sea.
>
> Two of us in the church-yard lie,
> My sister and my brother,
> And in the church-yard cottage, I
> Dwell near them with my mother."
>
> "You say that two at Conway dwell,
> And two are gone to sea,
> Yet you are seven; I pray you tell,
> Sweet Maid, how this may be?"
>
> Then did the little Maid reply,
> "Seven boys and girls are we;
> Two of us in the churchyard lie,
> Beneath the church-yard tree."
>
> "You run about, my little maid,
> Your limbs they are alive;

If two are in the church-yard laid,
Then ye are only five."

"Their graves are green, they may be seen,"
The little Maid replied,
"Twelve steps or more from my mother's door,
And they are side by side.

"My stockings there I often knit,
My kerchief there I hem;
And there upon the ground I sit
– I sit and sing to them.

And often after sunset, Sir,
When it is light and fair,
I take my little porringer,
And eat my supper there.

The first that died was little Jane;
In bed she moaning lay,
Till God released her of her pain,
And then she went away.

So in the church-yard she was laid,
And all the summer dry,
Together round her grave we played,
My brother John and I.

And when the ground was white with snow,
And I could run and slide,
My brother John was forced to go,
And he lies by her side."

"How many are you then," said I,
If they two are in Heaven?"
The little Maid did reply,
"O Master, we are seven."

"But they are dead; those two are dead!
Their spirits are in heaven!"
'Twas throwing words away; for still
The little Maid would have her will,
And said, "Nay, we are seven!"

I will start my reading by taking seriously Wordsworth's (1802) notion of 'ordinary things' [...] 'presented to the mind in an unusual aspect', because I think that there is something in this apparently comic yet artfully staged poetic exchange that renders unusual what we might otherwise quite ordinarily, if quietly, take for granted. I am referring here, as does de Bolla (2001), to the feeling that those who have died are not gone; that their absence, rather than leaving a gap or hole, is instead constitutive of presence, one that is as real as any living person. 'The fact that someone is dead', writes the novelist Julian Barnes (2014), 'may mean that they are not alive, but doesn't mean that they do not exist' (p. 102). Indeed, to feel and perhaps to exist in the continuing presence of the dead might be to 'admit' a kind of knowing or a kind of knowledge that differs significantly from the certainties insisted on by the adult in the poem. In part then, the drama of the poem turns on the little girl's conviction that 'we *are* seven' rather than we *were* seven, as a more biddable child might be persuaded to agree. Her belief in the continued presence of her unseen siblings is unshakeable; and it is this conviction that comes under increasing pressure from the adult who insists that the phrase 'we are seven' can and must refer only to those who are still alive.

This pressure begins with the opening stanza which is staged as a rhetorical address: 'A simple child [...] What should it know of death?' From the outset then, the reader is confronted with an ambiguity about whether death is something which a child *should* learn about as part of its ongoing education, or whether it is something that a child *could* even comprehend given its youth and immaturity. The poem's inquiry into this quandary proceeds via an interview couched in notably courteous terms. But despite his apparent civility, the inquisitor's twice-repeated use of the condescending phrase 'I pray you tell' suggests that something more than a casual question appears to be at stake. To 'tell', of course, commonly means to speak or to give an account of something. But it can also mean to count or give evidence as well as to disclose, reveal or predict. Indeed, we may 'tell the truth', but we can also 'tell tales', and the little girl in the poem turns out to be a 'teller' in rather more ways than one. Her 'telling' consists in using words that are true to the imaginative world in which she lives alongside a vivid sense of her dead brother and sister. Whilst her interrogator insists 'if two are in the churchyard laid/ Then ye are only five', 'the child herself quietly maintains that her dead siblings 'are' alive and present to her as much as her living brothers and sisters. 'Their graves are green, they may be seen' she protests, the slipperiness of the word 'they' here giving her interviewer leave to understand that it is her lost siblings, not merely their graves, that remain greenly alive and visible to her and to the world. But for her Gradgrindian inquisitor, 'telling' is constitutive of a demand that the child put away her childish imagination and adopt words that conform to what he sees as the facts of the matter.

But what is perhaps more telling for the reader is the way the adult's politeness starts to shift away from the terms of a conventional dialogue towards a rather more pressing kind of debate. Something closer to a Socratic interrogation gets under way in which the child's presumed false beliefs and unrecognised errors are to be remorselessly exposed via a particularly dogged kind of reasoning. In his well-known discourse of power, Socrates's knowledge and authority is always assumed from the start. The inquisitor in the poem – ironically, perhaps, addressed by the child initially as 'Sir' and finally as 'Master' – draws on the coercive power of age and experience to expose the fallibility of his young tutee's thinking and to bring her under the jurisdiction of his particular brand of rationality. For him, the dead John and Jane do not seem to count and his response to the child is determined by an entirely conventional understanding of death. But the little girl's love for her dead siblings goes further than the material reality before her; she sits and sings and eats her supper in what she believes to be the presence of her siblings, revealing an invisible and continuing bond that eludes the forced logic of the adult. The coerciveness here lies in the attempt to reduce the force of imagination to one of argumentation and in the expectation that the child will – must – succumb to what counts in the adult view of the world.

Concealed within this heavy-handed arithmetical debate I think lies a rather more substantive question about what in the poem counts – or 'tells' – as knowledge and who gets to decide. Counting itself has a rather ambiguous, not to say contradictory meaning here. In the world of the poem, it seems to refer to the way counting a person seems to reduce them to a number, an abstraction ('so ye are five') while simultaneously referring to the way in which someone who 'counts' might be thought to matter, to require attention like the dead Jane and John ('And there upon the ground I sit/I sit and sing to them'). Not to count, of course, is to be left out, forgotten or neglected; and in staging this debate, Wordsworth pits the child's capacity to know or 'count' something that the adult has ignored or perhaps long forgotten against the adult's all-too-knowing certainty about the facts of death and what 'counts' as real in the world. The adult's refusal to admit the child's imaginative kind of knowing is matched by the child's equally insistent refusal to admit the kind of conventional knowing that is being forced upon her. By maintaining an even-handed approach, then, the poem dramatises a hermeneutic dilemma in which the child's experience – conveyed by the repeated phrase 'we are seven' – is at odds with her interlocutor's different understanding of the very same words. It is tempting, of course, to take sides as Shokoff (1994) notes, and indeed many critical readings of this poem argue convincingly for the perspective adopted by one or other of the protagonists. But I want to suggest that our predicament as readers is one in which the need to take sides must be weighed against the value of maintaining the dilemma presented by the poem itself. For it is not (or not only) that the child's vision of the world is the result of an immature mind refusing to engage with an example of adult rationality; nor merely that a flat-footed adult is earnestly instructing a wise child in matters beyond her years. The little girl's resistance to acknowledging the adult's authoritative perspective is strangely matched by her simultaneous demand ('Nay, we are seven!') that her interrogator admit the validity of the version of the world *she* lives by. By placing these two visions of reality in contention, the poem's ironic force not only deconstructs the authority of the adult who seeks to dictate what constitutes knowledge in the world; it also thereby succeeds in deconstructing the authority of interpretation itself. By staging the language of authority, the adult's authority is revealed by the poem to be at least as much a fiction as is the imagined presence of the dead Jane and John in the mind of the little girl.

It is nonetheless true that we cannot help but find the little girl's assumptions about death far more interesting than the pedestrian views of her adult interlocutor; and it is clear that the child's perspective constitutes the real topic of the poem. But if we allow ourselves to examine her beliefs in the light of our own assumptions and views about death, we encounter what the little girl has to tell us in all its 'perplexity and obscurity'. Like the adult in the poem, we are stymied; we cannot know what she means, and we are not even helped here by trying to fathom what Wordsworth himself might have meant. The dilemma facing us in the poem seems to lie beyond authorial intention, constitutive of the much deeper linguistic and philosophical problem in literature concerning the relationship of words to experience. We might even say that one of the tasks undertaken by the poem is not to solve but rather to lay bare this dilemma by using the child's repetitive words 'we are seven' to convey a message that is not only subject to competing interpretations but is also only partially recoverable in words. In this way the poem seems to come up against its own limits, reduced like the adult, perhaps, to 'throwing words away'. Yet the words themselves testify to a kind of intractability, a certain resistance in which the phrase 'we are seven' comes to refuse or even exceed its semantic or syntactic meaning. It declares a knowledge that insists on concealing itself, an enigmatic knowing that stubbornly refuses any invitation to 'tell'.

'Confusion of the Tongues'

If psychoanalysis, like the poem, can be said to be preoccupied as much with hidden knowledge as the invitation to 'tell', we might with some justification wonder whether the kind of 'knowing' that is tied up in the poem's refusal has anything to tell us about the kind of 'knowing' that is bound up in the patient's resistance in psychoanalysis. I shall approach this rather complicated territory via de Bolla's (2001) wonderfully productive question about the difference it would make if the child in the poem were to acquiesce to the adult's demand for compliance. 'What would it mean', he asks, 'for the child to speak with the voice of the adult?' (p. 107). This, of course, is the very question that came to preoccupy Sandor Ferenczi, a colleague, analysand and devoted follower of Freud with whom he worked and corresponded throughout his life. In his clinical diary, Ferenczi leaves an intimate record of his struggle to manage this increasingly troubled relationship. In the final year of his life, it is clear he felt strongly that Freud had reverted to being an authoritative, scientific investigator, adopting an attitude of knowing superiority towards patients. 'Freud no longer loves his patients', he writes on May 1, 1932, 'he still remains attached to analysis intellectually, but not emotionally' (p. 93). In his final and controversial paper, 'Confusion of the Tongues between the Adults and the Child' presented in 1932 at the Congress of Wiesbaden, Ferenczi outlined his objections to what he saw as the prevailing sovereignty of the Freudian analyst whose interpretations he thought too readily violated the reality of the patient's experience. His antagonism is reserved for the traditional kind of transference interpretations favoured by Freud and his followers in which the analytic relationship is assumed to be a symbolic repetition of the patient's earlier significant attachment relationships. Revisiting Freud's (1896) abandoned seduction theory, Ferenczi controversially makes a plea for the analyst's recognition of the reality of childhood sexual abuse in the aetiology of neurosis instead of 'resorting prematurely to explanations – often too facile explanations – in terms of disposition and constitution' (p. 196).

Ferenczi's critique of these 'facile explanations' proposes a theory of childhood sexual trauma in which the child's 'language of tenderness' comes to be dominated by the adult's 'language of passion'; where an immature wish for 'tenderness' is wilfully misread by the adult as a wish for sexual 'passion'. In this 'confusion of the tongues', the abused child herself becomes 'tongue-tied' and unable to ask for help. A defensive identification subsequently ensues where the 'misused child changes into a mechanical, obedient automaton' (p. 202) due to the 'overpowering tone and authority of the adult'. A now ominous clinical outlook deteriorates further under the guise of a 'precocious maturity', in which the child's emotional and intellectual abilities are prematurely advanced in order to cope with the unspoken trauma. Ferenczi makes a reference here to the dream of the 'wise baby', drawing on his clinical experience of patients who dream about infants and young children who appear able to talk in learned, intellectual ways far beyond their years. In this dramatic illustration, more fully articulated in an earlier paper (Ferenczi 1923), a fear of losing tenderness from the adult is such that the sexually 'knowing' part of the child emerges in the form of a facsimile adult, one who might be supposed to know what has really happened and so come to the rescue. Ultimately, the child is destined to play the part of therapist or psychiatrist offering 'wisdom to the entire family' (p. 204).

We might see in Ferenczi's theory of seduction a partial, if literal, response to de Bolla's question about what would happen to the child in the poem if she were to conform to her interlocutor's arithmetic. But I want to develop my reading a bit further here because Ferenczi's most radical move is to link this 'confusion of the tongues' between adult and child with the 'confusion of the tongues' that can occur between psychoanalyst and patient in therapy. In this scenario, the intellectual explanations of the analyst come to dominate the patient, whose 'striking, almost helpless compliance' (p. 197) endorses the interpretations provided by the analyst. Just as the child's need for tenderness is usurped by the adult's wish for sexual passion, so too the patient's need to speak about the reality of her early abusive experience is usurped by the analyst's intellectual explanations. Indeed, Ferenczi goes further by suggesting that the analyst's 'cool educational attitude' (p. 200) actually provokes the very transference it claims to observe; and in this dismaying misreading of the patient's unconscious, any resistance to interpretation merely serves to confirm the validity of what the analyst already knows. Like Wordsworth's Socratic interlocutor, then, the analyst here attempts to coerce the patient into acknowledging the truth of what he says. A form of seduction gets under way in which the patient's 'exceedingly refined sensitivity for the wishes, tendencies, whims, sympathies and antipathies of their analyst' (p. 198) is unwittingly enrolled in the master-discourse of psychoanalysis and, like the 'wise baby' who caricatures the adult, learns to simulate its language. A theory of interpretation here thus collapses into a theory of seduction in which the reality of the patient's traumatic experience is violently subdued by the authoritative interpretations of the analyst: obedient agreement, even mimicry, appears to be constitutive of the 'talking cure'. In this disturbing clinical scene, the analyst refuses to acknowledge the resistance that lies concealed within the patient's quiet compliance, and complacently refuses the kind of self-knowing that might allow him to face the patient's 'hidden hatred and contempt' (p. 198). Like the adult in the poem, then, the analyst appears unable to 'admit' a certain kind of knowledge; perhaps he fails to remember what it is like to be a child and so his theoretical explanations might truly be said to be 'throwing words away'.

Our response to de Bolla's question seems to have developed somewhat, but in pushing the envelope of this inquiry a little further I can't help wondering if Wordsworth's poem can be brought to bear more fully on Ferenczi's ideas; and whether the kind of knowing conveyed by the little girl's repeated use of the phrase 'we are seven' can shed any further light on the malign transferential scene Ferenczi portrays. 'Is there repetition, or is there insistence? asks Gertrude Stein (1935); 'I am inclined to believe there is no such thing as repetition' (p. 288). There is certainly an increasingly insistent call for attention not only in the child's reiteration of her imaginative perspective, but also in the patient whose traumatic history repeats itself interminably within the transference. Ferenczi suggests that the patient's 'almost hallucinatory repetitions of traumatic experiences' (p. 197) emerge as a consequence of the analyst's overly-intellectualised theoretical explanations, mutely signalling a knowledge of the suffering for which she sought help in the first place. These repetitions only seem to grow more clamorous as they proceed. Ferenczi's patients apparently cause him a 'great deal of worry and embarrassment' (p. 197) just as the adult in the poem appears to feel increasingly agitated, even threatened, by the persistence of the little girl ('But they are dead; those two are dead!'). In both cases, a repeated demand for elucidation ('I pray you tell') yields an insistent 'telling' to which the interlocutors appear startlingly deaf.

Perhaps we can understand this deafness as one that is prefigured in the poem by the opening rhetorical address in which the question about what a child should know of death is posed. That there is an unknown and unknowable answer to this question makes the question itself not merely provocative, but cruel. Indeed, the poem is alive to the suffering inflicted by the failure to hear a child's perspective and the attempt to force her to 'tell' her story in the borrowed words of an adult. In part, this suffering is constituted by the adult's smug certainty, his intellectual 'fact-checking' and his determination to dress the child up in the garb of maturity. But the suffering within the poem – the suffering, I think, that the poem might be said to 'know' – goes much further. For the adult's repeated demands for elucidation are in the service of enforcing a view of the world in which there is no room for the little girl's dead siblings. The grief she feels at the loss of her brother and sister is thus intensified by the speaker's inability to acknowledge and validate the way she is trying to make good her traumatic losses. And when we, as readers, try to clarify what the little girl means – what *does* she really know of death, after all? – perhaps we too risk imposing the very pain the adult cannot help but inflict. Our call for enlightenment, like his, has the effect of drawing attention to that which seemingly cannot be heard at all and which therefore can never fully be known. By insisting that the little girl 'tells' of something that cannot be put into words, the poem sets out to stage the very limits of a language it must perforce use itself. I think this might be what de Bolla (2001) means by his enigmatic statement that the poem itself is 'the cause of the hurt it seeks to uncover and to heal' (p. 118), as if the impossible quest for meaning in the poem opens up a wound within the recesses of language that the poem strives both to reveal and repair. In this provocative idea I suspect there is much that speaks to psychoanalysis. For in this 'confusion of the tongues' that Ferenczi identifies there is surely a wound too: a hurt inflicted by the demand that the patient put words to her unutterable trauma. In his masterful quest for clarification, in his determined attempts to dress the patient up in his own theoretical language, the analyst elicits the 'dumb show' of hysteria: the patient's unconscious repetition of a suffering of which she knows but cannot tell, a suffering that the analyst can only cure by recourse to further words.

By inflicting the very pain they set out to cure, both literature and psychoanalysis might be said to open up and expose us to suffering; and in seeking words that are, as the Greek poet George Seferis says, 'strong enough to help', both find a way to address what Seamus Heaney (1995) calls 'the complex burden of our own experience' (p. 10). The word 'burden', whose dictionary definition includes 'that which is borne, a load', is a term usually taken to refer to a labour, a duty or responsibility. So perhaps I can lean on Heaney's phrase here to advance the idea that the work of both the writer and the analyst is the kind that entails bearing a certain responsibility, a complex duty that constitutes what we might call its emotional 'load'. For the words of the patient in analysis, like the words of the poem, conceal a particular kind of knowing, an experience that can never fully be articulated, accessed or released. The burden of both psychoanalysis and literature could then be said to hold, understand and keep safe the incommunicado nature of this 'knowing' even as they seek its fullest possible expression. Indeed, it seems to me that in a very difficult way both the writer and the psychoanalyst must thereby also bear the burden of a sense of guilt which they will continually labour to redress. For in a 'reaching-out toward expression', as Robert Frost (1923) says, in summoning our sustained awareness of an intense emotional experience, both might be said to inspire a quest for meaning that cannot be satisfied, a longing for that which cannot be known.

Conclusion

The idea that there is a wound within literature and psychoanalysis, that both might stimulate a desire they cannot fulfil, I think constitutes the healing ground common to both disciplines. If the task of addressing 'the complex burden of our own experience' falls, albeit in different ways, to both literary fiction and psychoanalysis then perhaps we might conclude it is time for each discipline to recognise the other in this shared endeavour. So I want to concur with psychoanalytic literary critics such as Felman (1977) who argue that any dialogue between the two fields needs to take place outside the Hegelian 'fight for recognition' where the explanatory force and conceptual vocabulary of psychoanalysis is granted a privileged position over literature and where literature is expected to take up an ancillary relationship to psychoanalytic knowledge. It may be that finding ways to resist rather than collude with what Felski (2015) calls the 'violence of interpretation' may turn out to be one of the main aims of this book. But just as writers such as Wood (2005) and de Bolla (2001) usefully personify literary fiction and what it can be considered to 'know', too we might want to register the implied anthropomorphism in Felman's notion of 'recognition'. For the term 'recognition' refers first and foremost to a sense of mutuality occurring between people, and only in a very secondary sense, if at all, to mutuality between disparate professional disciplines. To recognise and be recognised refers to the way we are, as Butler (2004) writes, '[g]iven over from the start to the world of others' (p. 26), constituted by our attachments and a primary relationality that is the social condition of our formation as subjects. To draw further on the metaphor of 'recognition' then, is to understand that however we may conceive the nature of the relationship between literature and psychoanalysis, we need to acknowledge the existence of a somewhat ambivalent attachment between the two disciplines that have been involved, embroiled and implicated with each other now for over a century; and that it might be worth our while, as Felman (1977) goes on to suggest, 'to explore, bring to light and articulate the various (indirect) ways in which the two domains do indeed implicate each other' (p. 9).

In the borrowed words of the poem, then, let us ask: what should psychoanalysis know of literature? What should literature know of psychoanalysis?

These are questions, I suggest, that relate to attitude, to stance and to the way mutual recognition can only properly be conferred on the basis of a shared wound, a shared vulnerability. But a 'fight for recognition' implies a struggle for power in which the authority of one always threatens to prevail over the other. It is an imagined contest that presupposes a wish for invulnerability, a defensive stance indexing a wound that dare not be exposed. Psychoanalysis, like the adult in the poem who looks down condescendingly on the little girl, perhaps too easily adopts a position of interpretative mastery; and literary fiction, like the child whose oblique gaze identifies something her adult interlocutor cannot fathom, too readily occupies the place of an ironic, critical aside. But recognition I think implies a face-to-face meeting, a courageous willingness for each, if only momentarily, to expose and be exposed to the vulnerability of the other and in that encounter to thereby be challenged and changed. To petition for mutual recognition here would not only invite psychoanalysis and literature to affirm and celebrate each other's specialist methods and modes of knowledge; it would also solicit a future in which both these disciplines bear witness to a way of knowing that announces the limits of its own authority, that resists as inappropriate the language of explanation and speaks its hidden truths softly, even in the voice of a little child.

References

Attridge, D. (2009). On knowing works of art. In: C. Birdsall, M. Boletsi, I. Sapir and P. Verstraete (eds), *Inside Knowledge: (Un)doing Ways of Knowing in the Humanities*, pp. 17–34. Newcastle-upon-Tyne: Cambridge Scholars Publishing.
Barnes, J. (2014). *Levels of Life*. London: Vintage.
Barthes, R. (1977). Lecture in Inauguration of the Chair of Literary Semiology. *College de France*, October, 8: 3–16.
Brooks, P. (1987). The idea of a psychoanalytic literary criticism. *Critical Inquiry*, 13, 2: 334–348.
Butler, J. (2004). *Precarious Life. The Powers of Mourning and Violence*. London: Verso.
de Bolla, P. (2001). *Art Matters*. Cambridge, MA: Harvard University Press.
Eysenck, H. (1985). *Decline and Fall of the Freudian Empire*. London: Taylor and Francis.
Felman, S. (1977). To open the question. *Yale French Studies*, No. 55–6: 5–10.
Felski, R. (2015). *The Limits of Critique*. Chicago: The University of Chicago Press.
Felski, R. (2020). *Hooked: Art and Attachment*. Chicago: The University of Chicago Press.
Ferenczi, S. (1923). The dream of the 'clever baby'. In Ferenczi (1926), *Further Contributions to the Theory and Technique of Psychoanalysis*, pp. 349–350. London: Hogarth Press.
Ferenczi, S. (1932). Confusion of the tongues between the adults and the child: the language of tenderness and of passion. Reprinted in: *Contemporary Psychoanalysis* (1988), 24: 196–206.
Freud, S. (1896/2004). *Studies in Hysteria*. London: Penguin.
Freud, S. (1910). Wild analysis. In: Peter Gay (ed.), *The Freud Reader*, pp. 351–356. London: Vintage.
Frosh, S. (2010). *Psychoanalysis Outside the Clinic: Interventions in Psychosocial Studies*. Basingstoke: Palgrave Macmillan.

Frost, R. (1923). In: H. Holt (ed.), *Robert Frost: the Man and his Work*. New York: Henry Holt.
Gourgouris, S, (2003). *Does Literature Think?* Stanford, CA: Stanford University Press.
Grunbaum, A. (1984). *The Foundations of Psychoanalysis: a Philosophical Critique*. Berkeley and Los Angeles: University of California Press.
Habermas, J. (1971). *Knowledge and Human Interests*. London: Heinemann.
Heaney, S. (1995). *The Redress of Poetry*. London: Faber and Faber.
Hoffman, I. (2009). Doublethinking our way to scientific legitimacy: the dessication of human experience. *Journal of the American Psychoanalytic Association*, 1043–1069.
Kazin, A. (1961). The language of pundits. *The Atlantic*, July.
Macherey, P. (1990). *Literature in the Modern World*. Oxford: Oxford University Press.
Nussbaum, M. (1990). *Love's Knowledge. Essays on Philosophy and Literature*. New York: Oxford University Press.
Ogden, B. H. and Ogden, T. H. (2012). How the analyst thinks as clinician and as literary reader. *Psychoanalytic Perspectives*, 9: 243–273.
Phillips, A. (2002). *Promises Promises. Essays on Literature and Psychoanalysis*. London: Faber and Faber.
Ricoeur, P. (1970). *Freud and Philosophy: An Essay on Interpretation*, trans. Denis Savage. New Haven, CT: Yale University Press.
Sedgwick, E. (1997). Paranoid reading and reparative reading; or, you're so paranoid, you probably think this introduction is about you. In: *Novel Gazing: Queer Readings in Fiction*. Durham, NC and London: Duke University Press.
Shokoff, J. (1994). Wordsworth's duty as a poet in "We Are Seven" and "Surprised by Joy". *The Journal of English and Germanic Philology*, 93, 2:228–239.
Stein, G. (1935). Portraits and repetition. In: *Stein. Writings 1932–1946*, pp. 287–312. Penguin Group USA, 2001.
Wallerstein, R. (2009). What kind of research in psychoanalysis? *International Journal of Psycho-Analysis*, 90: 109–133.
Walsh, D. (1969). *Literature and Knowledge*. Middletown, CT: Wesleyan University Press.
Wood, M. (2005). *Literature and the Taste of Knowledge*. New York: Cambridge University Press.
Woolf, V. (1925). *Mrs Dalloway*. London: Penguin English Library, 2018.
Wordsworth, W. (2008). *The Prose Works*, ed. W. Owen and J. Smyser. Humanities E-books, LLP.
Wordsworth, W. (1802). *The Rainbow*.
Wordsworth and Coleridge: Lyrical Ballads 1798 and 1802, ed. F. Stafford (2013). Oxford: Oxford University Press.

Chapter 1

Copying, cloning and creativity
Kazuo Ishiguro's *Never Let Me Go*

> Imitation cannot go above its model.
> (Ralph Waldo Emerson, Divinity School Address 1838)

Introduction

Growing up in 1970s London, I wanted to be a violinist. When I was nine years old, my parents bought me a cheap violin and I started, very painfully, to master the difficult art of making the kind of sound that other people could bear to listen to. Later, as a teenager training to be a violinist, I was enthralled to hear a piece of violin music written by the early 20th century Viennese composer/violinist Fritz Kreisler, and I immediately went off to my local library – no smartphones or digital streaming in those days! – to see if I could find more. Eventually, I located an early recording of Kreisler himself playing his own compositions: *Liebesleid, Liebesfreud, Schön Rosmarin, Tambourin Chinois, Praeludium and Allegro, Humoresque*, miniature gems that sparkled through the hiss and crackle on my old family gramophone. I listened to them avidly. But what mesmerised me was not only the music; it was the quality of the sound that Kreisler drew from his violin, a quality that even now I can conjure up in my mind, its precise tone and timbre utterly distinctive, like a fingerprint. Smoky, woody, mellow, warm and flavoursome, Kreisler's inimitable sound was redolent of a faded but fascinating and romantic fin-de-siècle Viennese era that I knew nothing of, but was utterly enchanted by. The sound of his violin was like chocolate cream. I wanted to eat him up.

And indeed, I proceeded to eat him up over a period of several years. Hour after hour, week in, week out, after school and at weekends, I was listening to his records over and over again. My ears became a conduit through which I was absorbing sheer magic. I thought that if I heard it for long enough – and if I practised hard enough – then, surely, that same enchantment, now installed within the bones and cartilage of my ears, would somehow flow out through my fingers and bow, replicating the rich, sophisticated sensuousness that Kreisler incarnated for me at that time. Years later, with all that practice,

DOI: 10.4324/9781003325468-2

I got to play some of those wonderful pieces myself. But what I really sought, more than anything else, was to draw the same quality of sound from my own little violin and to cast that magic spell myself: to make my violin sing in the way that Kreisler's did. I wanted to charm, mesmerise and enthral those who were listening to me in the same way as he had captivated his audiences. Such hubris could never succeed of course. It was only later as an adult, long after I had given up my dream of becoming a violinist, that I came to recognise how important it had been for me to try to imitate that fabulous sound. My protracted efforts to absorb, ingest, soak up Kreisler until he actually became part of me, part of my very cell structure, I now see as an early attempt at creatively establishing a sound for myself, an effort to find my own musical voice through the voice of another.

'Identification', says Fuss (1995), 'is that detour through the other that defines a self' (p. 2). Unwittingly, we absorb aspects of each other, unconsciously incorporating the tone, the flavour, the characteristics and mannerisms, the emotional stamp of the other whose ghostly presence becomes threaded through the fabric of our own subjectivity. Self-identity presupposes, is predicated on, a kind of permeability. Indeed, this extraordinary psychological porousness, says Freud (1921) 'is the earliest and original form of emotional tie [...] the ego assumes the characteristic of the object' (p. 107). In 1917, Freud had already discussed how, in melancholia, the ego identifies with the lost object, in this way magically retaining and preserving its link to the absent person. He was subsequently to see in this elegiac process of ego formation a more general feature of the individual's development: 'The character of the ego', he writes in 1923, 'is a precipitate of abandoned object cathexes and [...] it contains the history of those object choices' (p. 29). We are all, according to Freud, in thrall to, appropriated by the other, and this insertion of the other into the self is constitutive. At its inauguration, the self is signed and sealed, as it were, by its commemorative ties to the other.

As a psychologist and psychoanalyst, I have always been fascinated by these themes of identification and copying. Perhaps this is why I have been drawn to the notion of the clone, that literary device so frequently used to explore and interrogate notions of identity and selfhood. In 1932, Huxley took up the idea in *Brave New World* by describing his concept of 'Bokanovsky's process' where human embryos are split to produce identical gamma, delta and epsilon drones, engineered to perform menial labour for the superior alphas and betas. Later writers, such as Alvin Toffler (1970) in *Future Shock* and Ira Levin (1976) in *The Boys from Brazil*, wrote about a future where human beings would be able to make carbon copies of themselves. Kazuo Ishiguro's (2005) sixth novel *Never Let Me Go* offers a dystopian myth that interrogates the nature of time, memory and creativity using the fiction of an artificially-generated group of children without origins who are manufactured in order to sacrifice their body parts for others. In his bleakly beautiful tragedy, Ishiguro raises multiple ethical, spiritual and psychological issues, woven into a restrained and moving exploration of what Dennett (1976) has called 'conditions of personhood'.

Like the novelist, we might think of the psychoanalyst too as someone who is concerned with 'conditions of personhood': with illuminating and describing the ways in which we are constituted as subjects, as well as with the difficulties of recognising the other as subject in his or her own right. Indeed, the multitude of psychoanalytic terms and theories attempting to label and account for the process of identity formation is testament to our difficulties in articulating exactly how we develop and evolve a sense of self in relation to others. I want to approach this admittedly complex topic via a reading of Ishiguro's novel, using his story of cloned children to explore the significance of copying and creativity in the development of self-hood. Along the way, I will try to develop my thinking with reference to notions of time, memory and translation, drawing on work by Freud, Laplanche and Walter Benjamin as well as Emily Apter's recent ideas about textual translation.

Never Let Me Go[1]

Ishiguro's novel revolves round the first-person narrative testimony of Kathy H., a 31-year-old woman remembering a childhood spent at a boarding school called Hailsham. Although we are told this was in England in the 'late 1990s', it soon becomes clear that Kathy inhabits a world that only partially parallels the liberal, democratic Britain with which we are familiar. Indeed, from the outset, the reader is presented with a number of puzzling anomalies, of which Kathy's incomplete name, raising questions about her lineage and background, is only the first. For like all the other children at Hailsham along with her friends Ruth and Tommy, Kathy appears to have no home or parents of her own. The teachers who look after the children are referred to as 'guardians' and they, in turn, are called 'normals' by the children. Inhabiting the limited awareness of the children, the reader only gradually comes to understand that their lives are dictated by the circumstances of their status as infertile clones. They have been created by scientific technology to service 'normals' in an outside world that requires their organs for medical treatment. At sixteen, they will leave Hailsham and spend some time in an intermediate establishment before being called up, at first to be 'carers' for other 'donors', and then to start donating themselves. Their lives are destined to be cut short. After the fourth operation to harvest the last of their vital organs, they are likely to die in their thirties; or rather, in the euphemistic language of the guardians, they will 'complete'. Only Miss Lucy, one of the guardians at Hailsham, is prepared to hint at what is to come:

> The problem, as I see it, is that you've been told and not told. You've been told, but none of you really understand, and I dare say, some people are quite happy to leave it that way. But I'm not. If you're going to have decent lives, then you've got to know and know properly. None of you will go to America, none of you will be film stars. And none of you will

> be working in supermarkets as I heard some of you planning the other day. Your lives are set out for you. You'll become adults, then before you're old, before you're even middle-aged, you'll start to donate your vital organs. That's what each of you was created to do. You're not like the actors you watch on your videos, you're not even like me. You were brought into this world for a purpose, and your futures, all of them, have been decided.
>
> (p. 73)

While there has been much disagreement about the genre of *Never Let Me Go*, it is apparent very early on in the story that it is not a traditional science-fiction novel. Ishiguro makes no attempt to engage with scientific or ethical debates about reproductive technology. Indeed, he is portraying a world in which ethical issues and concerns about bioengineering and cloning appear already to have been resolved, regulated and normalised; a world in which the children's lack of legitimate origins and reproductive capacity renders them expendable in the eyes of 'normals'. Against this surreal backdrop, the void, the aching emptiness and the sense of dimly-glimpsed loss at the heart of the children's lives is only slowly and incrementally revealed. Like the children themselves, we are 'told and not told'. The pace of our understanding is rationed, not because Ishiguro is a latter-day Agatha Christie, but because he wants us to inhabit his characters' gradually dawning awareness of their fate. References are oblique, visible only in the characters' actions and voiced in a deceptively understated prose. Through the lens of Kathy's evolving memories, we only gradually begin to realise the significance of the narrated events and the reasons why the children are viewed by 'normals' as different. It is through her partial disclosures, digressions and mistaken deductions that we slowly begin to detach from Kathy's naïve perspective and eventually arrive at a fuller picture of the children's circumstances and the dreadful realities of their foreshortened futures. Ishiguro's trademark unreliable narrator here becomes less an occasion for irony than for growing compassion as we follow Kathy in her puzzled attempts to interrogate her memory and to understand her earlier life at Hailsham with Ruth and Tommy.

We learn that the position of the students at Hailsham is one that is not only predicated on and constituted by loss; it is one that encompasses a profound discarding of their subjectivity. This theme is indexed by Ishiguro's quiet but repeated allusion to the role of rubbish, its textual unobtrusiveness mirroring the children's occluded awareness of their status as disposable items themselves. The assortment of toys and clothes that are brought to the school for the excitedly-anticipated 'Sales' are all items the children are encouraged to buy with 'tokens' that are provided by the school. It is clear, however, that it is the 'Sales' themselves that are token; not only because there is no true financial exchange involved, but because what is 'sold' consists only of things that have been rejected or discounted by people living in the outside world. Similarly, the

'Exchanges' that take place between students four times a year – mirroring the four 'donations' that they will all be expected to make before 'completing' – involve 'buying' each other's paintings and sculptures made from old bits of trash and garbage such as bottle tops and crushed tin cans: a recycling of personal possessions that foreshadows the future recycling of their own body parts.

Within this desolate setting, Ishiguro draws attention to the role of art as signifier of the very interiority that the children are assumed to lack. Art is valued highly at Hailsham; and the mysterious Madame who visits the school selects and removes the children's best creations. Not understanding why their artwork is taken away, Kathy starts to pick up stories from other students as well as snippets from her teachers, eventually piecing together a story about Madame's 'Gallery' which is stocked with the children's art in order to prove to the outside world that they have souls. The hypothetical status of the Gallery – 'everyone talked about it as though it existed, though in truth none of us knew for certain that it did' (p. 28) – mirrors the uncertain ontological status of the children and the perpetual question-mark that hovers over the existence and validity of their inner worlds.

The unstated losses that reverberate through this novel are embodied by two central interrelated fantasies that come to dominate the children's lives. The first is a fantasy among all the pupils at Hailsham about lost property. What the children call light-heartedly the 'lost corner' in the school is the place they go to if they lose a jumper or a book, or if they find anyone else's possessions. But hearing in a geography lesson about Norfolk, the 'lost corner' of England, the children develop a story among themselves about how this place is where all the lost things in life end up. Norfolk comes to assume a mythical, Atlantis-like status in their imaginations; in the face of the children's loss of home and their lack of a sense of belonging, it becomes not only a site of lost hopes but also a location of future fulfilment. Indeed, in adulthood, as Ruth awaits her final 'donation', she is consoled by this reassuring idea that 'when we lost something precious, and we'd looked and looked and still couldn't find it, then we didn't have to be completely heartbroken [...] we could always go and find it again in Norfolk' (p. 61).

Norfolk turns out to be the place where the now teenaged children are sent after they finish their education at Hailsham. The Cottages are a kind of halfway home where they are permitted a little more freedom before being called up to start donating their body parts. It is here that Ruth and Tommy begin a romantic relationship, leaving Kathy, who loves and understands Tommy, to manage her jealousy and her own sexual yearnings. It is at this point the second fantasy, the myth of the 'possible', is elaborated:

> Since each of us was copied at some point from a normal person, there must be, for each of us, somewhere out there, a model getting on with his or her life. This meant, at least in theory, you'd be able to find the person you were modelled from. That's why, when you went out there

yourself – in the towns, shopping centres, transport cafés – you kept an eye out for 'possibles' – the people who might have been the models for you and your friends.

(p. 127)

Kathy's studiedly bland voice here disguises Ishiguro's penetrating rendition of the orphan's desperate search for the lost parent. In the absence of a narrative of origins, of belonging, the children try to invent their pasts by speculating about the human model from which they believe they were derived. In this way, they also create a narrative about the kind of life they have the potential to lead and the kind of person they would like to become. Hearing from some friends that a 'model' for Ruth has been spotted in nearby Cromer, Ruth, Tommy and Kathy decide to visit the town to see for themselves if this is really Ruth's 'possible'. Glimpsing a woman through the glass door of an office they follow her with excitement and trepidation as she walks to a public art gallery. It is in this gallery, not coincidentally among the pictures and works of art that announce the presence of interiority in 'normals', they all begin to realise that this woman cannot be Ruth's 'possible'. Her physical presence and voice appear to be 'closer that we'd ever really wanted' (p. 149), and in the face of such proximity the mirage of the 'possible' rapidly recedes. As they all leave the gallery, Ruth's disappointment and disillusion are palpable. Rejecting all comfort from her friends, she violently dismisses the idea that they could ever be modelled from someone 'normal'. 'If you want to look for possibles', she angrily insists, 'if you want to do it properly, then you look in the gutter. You look in rubbish bins. Look down the toilet' (p. 152).

But the visit to the 'lost corner' of England is to yield something of value after all. After Ruth storms off, Tommy and Kathy start to investigate the local shops. They are hunting for a precious cassette tape that was stolen from Kathy at Hailsham some years previously. The tape is a copy of a recording made by the fictitious 1950s nightclub singer Judy Bridgewater, a song that Kathy used to play over and over again as a pupil in the school. Its lyrics express her unspoken, unfulfillable yearning to experience an intimate connection with a mother and, in turn, to hold close a baby to which she herself will never be able to give birth: '[W]hat I'd imagined was a woman who'd been told she couldn't have babies, who'd really, really wanted them all her life. Then there's a sort of miracle and she has a baby and she holds this baby very close to her and walks around singing: 'Baby, never let me go…' partly because she's so happy, but also because she's so afraid something will happen, that the baby will get ill or be taken away from her' (p. 64).

Rummaging among the odds and ends in a nearby jumble shop, Kathy and Tommy eventually locate the lost recording in a heap of recycled rubbish. The discovery of the cassette tape provides the hope they need to cement and develop the love they have always had for each other. It is at this point the pre-ordained lives of the three main characters now inexorably gather momentum. Over the next few months, Ruth will be 'called up' to donate and soon Tommy, too, starts to undergo operations while Kathy's role remains, for the moment at least, that of gifted 'carer'. Having been disillusioned about ever finding their 'possibles', Kathy and Tommy subsequently desperately seek more time to be together before they too succumb to their fate. Having heard a rumour in Hailsham that those who are truly in love can seek a 'deferral' before they have to start donating their organs, Tommy suggests that they need to find their old guardians at Hailsham, to ask whether this is true.

But the unavoidable realities of Kathy and Tommy's existence are driven home when they eventually locate Madame and Miss Emily. In a final conversation with them, the terrible contingencies of the children's lives are laid bare. Hailsham turns out to have been at the forefront of social reforms in the care of cloned children: a unique social experiment in which, as Madame and Miss Emily explain, 'we demonstrated to the world that if students were reared in humane, cultivated environments, it was possible for them to grow to be as sensitive and intelligent as any ordinary human being' (p. 239). The guardians attempt to exonerate themselves, telling Kathy and Tommy it is because of Hailsham that they and their friends have managed to lead good, educated and cultured lives. They make it clear they always had the children's best interests at heart; that it would have done no good to burden them with the knowledge of what was to come. Indeed, the meeting only serves to underline the fact that there is no more time for Kathy and Tommy: no deferral of their fate. Their lives have been a product of the outside world's interests and they must now live out the purpose for which they were born. Finally, Madame tells Kathy that she remembers seeing her as a little girl, singing to herself along with the cassette tape, and explains how she felt:

> I saw a new world coming rapidly. More scientific, efficient, yes. More cures for the old sicknesses. Very good. But a harsh, cruel world. And I saw a little girl, her eyes tightly closed, holding to her breast the old kind world, one that she knew in her heart could not remain, and she was holding it and pleading, never to let her go.
>
> (p. 248–9)

In the bleakest of conclusions, Kathy and Tommy are left to return home so that Tommy can undergo a final donation before he 'completes'. Kathy herself remains a carer to the end, awaiting the moment when she too will be forced to start sacrificing her own organs.

Copying and cloning

Copying, of course, is something we cannot help doing. The capacity for imitation seems central to notions of what we think it means to be human. 'It is an instinct of human beings, from childhood, to engage in mimesis,' writes

Aristotle, 'indeed, this distinguishes them from other animals: man is the most mimetic of all, and it is through mimesis that he develops his earliest understandings' (2005, p. 38). Perhaps it is for this reason that psychoanalysis has always had theories about copying. Probably the best known of these is the Winnicottian distinction between the 'true' and the 'false' self. While the true self is based on an experience or an illusion of omnipotence provided by the 'good enough' mother, the false self derives from a failure of such an illusion and results in the precocious use of the mind as an alternative to dependence on a reliable caretaker. Over time, the false self starts to dominate, with compliance as 'the main feature, with imitation as a speciality' (Winnicott. 1960, p. 147). Identification, then, seems to replace authenticity – 'There may', admits Winnicott, 'be some almost personal living through imitation' – but the infant has now been seduced into a kind of pretence, a facsimile existence where he or she has to comply with what is required and identify with – become 'like' – the person who appears to be in charge.

Ishiguro has always been interested in the various ways in which we become 'like' someone else. His strategies of description and narration frequently mime the characteristics of British people and their culture, something most fully realised in the creation of Stevens, the English butler in his 1989 novel *The Remains of the Day*. Ishiguro's interest in simulation follows a different trajectory in *Never Let Me Go*, where the cloned children's very existence is predicated on imitation. Born without parents, they have no alternative but to conform unquestioningly to the rules and mores of Hailsham. With no friends or family in the outside world, they are forced to understand people and make relationships by copying the behaviour, mannerisms and gestures of each other and from those they watch on TV. As Kathy tells Ruth, who has picked up a way of slapping Tommy on the arm, a habit she has learned from her friends who themselves have acquired it from a television comedy: 'It's not what people really do out there in normal life [...] It looks daft, the way you copy everything they do' (p. 113). These second-hand gestures and behaviours, akin to the second-hand cassette tapes, toys and objects they receive in the 'Sales', are mirrored by the flat, bland, apparently untroubled voice of Kathy. While some, such as Frank Kermode (2005), have critiqued the deceptively simple, 'chatty', first-person narrative style of *Never Let Me Go*, we might instead understand it as an evocation of the constraints and mimetic conditions of Kathy's very existence. The clichés and colloquialisms she deploys articulate her experience in the manner of a schoolgirl who can only express herself by copying the words and jargon she hears around her.

The idea that humans are themselves copiers in much the same way as are clones allows Ishiguro to destabilise any clear distinction between the two. Indeed, I suggest the blurring of the boundary between clones and 'normals' in *Never Let Me Go* ensures that the very category of originality and the essentialism it implies is contested. Kathy and her friends, along with Madame, privilege the idea of a unique individuality, something assumed to be possessed by 'normals' in the world. It is this Romantic logic that underpins the myth of the 'possible: 'when you saw the person you were copied from, you'd get *some* insight into who you were deep down, and maybe too, you'd see something of what your life held in store' (p. 127). Uniqueness here is prized as an ontological given, defining not only who a person is but what they will become; it denotes their value and significance in the eyes of the world. Believing in the existence of a 'possible' means that the cloned children assume they only accrue value on the basis of the prior existence of a person from whom their DNA was taken. This myth becomes the vehicle through which Ishiguro pushes us to interrogate exactly what it is that makes an individual unique. Does it depend on the existence of a prior original? Or can it be attributed to something else?

Perhaps we can thicken the discussion here by drawing an analogy with the relationship of a translation to an original or primary text. There are well-known limits to our capacity to render a primary text into another language. Despite the translator's best attempts to ensure the latter's correspondence to the former, to 'copy' it as it were, it is impossible to retain absolute fidelity to the original's language and meaning. There can be no exact word-for-word equivalent to the source text; indeed, it is for this reason that the Italian epigram so bluntly states '*traduttore, traditore*': to translate is to betray. Paz (1971) points out the medium that makes translation possible – i.e. language – is already itself a translation: 'first from the nonverbal world and then because each sign and each phrase is a translation of another sign, another phrase' (p. 154). So in the shifting process of translation, there is always something untranslatable left over: a stubborn core of semantic incommensurability that flatly resists any attempt at equivalence or substitution.

But what happens when it is not the translation but rather the source text itself that is called into question? Emily Apter's (2006) work in the field of translation has led her to explore some of the ethical and epistemological issues that arise in those instances of translations that either pretend or are taken to be an original work. In her discussion of historical cases of literary fraud, Apter argues that allegations of 'pseudotranslation' are significant neither because they expose literary scandals about forgery and 'authorial counterfeit' (p. 213), nor because they reveal previously hidden criteria relating to the value and status of original works of literature. Rather, they lay bare the uncertainty regarding the translated text's ontological status: whether it is born from a 'real' original, authenticated work by a known author, or whether it is engineered from a 'kind of "test tube text" of simulated originality' (p. 213). The possibility of a text that is 'unnaturally, or artificially birthed and successfully replicated' (p. 213) confronts the reader, she suggests, 'with a situation in which the translation mislays the original, absconding to some other world of textuality that retains the original only as fictive pretext' (p. 212).

Apter's discussion of the textual 'cloning' that can occur in translation offers a startling parallel to the dilemma with which Ishiguro confronts the children. For *Never Let Me Go* seems to be a story not so much about a scandalous political plot to harvest organs from cloned children; nor is it merely a tale that sets out to expose the invisible yardstick used by society to judge an individual's humanity. Rather, we might think of Ishiguro's tale as one that turns a tender gaze upon the fragility and ambiguity of the clones' ontological status. Like Apter's translation without an original, the children are faced with the task of living a life in which they have been 'artificially birthed and successfully replicated'. They too have mislaid their origins; and in these circumstances, they invent the 'fictive pretext' of the 'possible' in order to sustain the notion that there was such an original in existence. It enables them to maintain the idea that they derive from someone who was born with an ontologically valuable interior: a fantasy that allows them to believe they too possess interiority and hence a capacity for artistic originality and authentic love. Only then, the children believe, will they finally achieve the status and value of 'normals' in the world. It is hardly surprising then, as Apter points out, that the notion of a translation without an original raises ethical and ontological questions; for if the translation is not that which is based on an original source, what is it?

Time, memory, translation

Ishiguro invites the reader to consider this question and join the children on their search for self-understanding and identity by means of a narrative deploying flashbacks, hindsight and memories. But memories are not isomorphic with events. When we remember the past, we are not simply retrieving the unvarnished facts of a situation. 'Our memories are card-indexes consulted', grumbles Cyril Connolly (1944), 'and then put back in disorder by authorities whom we do not control' (p. 84). Laplanche's name for this disorder – his French translation, in fact, of Freud's (1918) notion of Nachträglichkeit – was 'après-coup' or 'afterwardsness', a somewhat awkward expression denoting the way in which prior events come to acquire meaning and significance through the retrospective action of memory. Just as Kathy is revisiting, rethinking and retrieving the events of her childhood at Hailsham in the light of subsequent events, so too Laplanche (1999) suggests: 'The subject revises past events at a later date [nachträglich] and that it is the revision which invests them with significance and even with efficacity of pathogenic force' (p. 112).

Laplanche was trying to resolve a long-standing psychoanalytic dilemma: whether the past determines the present – as in Freud's defence of the 'real' primal scene in his case history of the 'Wolf Man' – or whether the present retroactively determines the past, via reconstruction of prior events that come to acquire the status of truth for the individual. Laplanche's position points to the importance of the adult's message – the 'enigmatic signifier' as he calls it – that is implanted into the individual, the child, and the way in which subsequently that unconscious message will always be translated and reinterpreted: 'This past', he argues, cannot be a purely factual one, an unprocessed or raw 'given'. It contains rather in an immanent fashion something that comes before – a message from the other. It is impossible therefore to put forward a purely hermeneutic position on this – that is to say, that everyone interprets their past according to their present – because the past already has something deposited in it that demands to be deciphered, which is the message of the other person.

(1999, p. 265)

As children, then, we cannot help but assimilate the enigmatic, traumatising, unspoken messages conveyed by the adult. Like Kathy and her friends at Hailsham, we are all, somehow, 'told and not told'. We have no means of understanding or translating what has been unconsciously conveyed to us, even though, as Tommy says, '[a]t some level you always knew'. It is the residue of these untranslatable communications that forms the core of the child's own unconscious and which he or she continuously attempts to master, reinterpret and retranslate. The shudder that Madame is always suppressing in the children's presence, for example, is emblematic of the tacit message that they are somehow different, repulsive, abject; it is an unconscious communication the children attempt to master and represent via their artwork and the redemptive potential they believe it holds for them. But in this model of the self, it is not simply the unconscious of the child that is at stake; for the adult who implants these enigmatic messages is equally unconscious of what he or she is doing to the child and of what is being conveyed. This means that there is no clear relationship between the parental unconscious and the child's, no direct relationship between the past and the present; there is instead, as Laplanche (1999) suggests, a 'profound reshaping' that occurs between the two. In adulthood, we will continue unconsciously to rework and revise the messages or memories that we have already attempted to translate during childhood; indeed, we can only ever translate our translations, as it were. It is as if we thought we were pressing the 'save' function on the computer keyboard, whereas we now realise were always pressing 'save as'. As Modell (1999) suggests, our memories are constantly in the process of being overwritten, rethought and re-invented throughout our lifetime.

What is interesting about this translation model of the unconscious is that it unsettles what we mean by an original, correct, 'true' memory as much as it debunks any notion of an original or 'true' self. Indeed, like Apter's (2006) notion of a translation without textual predicate, it suggests that in questions of personal identity there may be no original, privileged or Winnicottian 'true' self to refer back to, but only a series of translations or versions of the self which now assume priority. In this apparent reversal of the traditional hierarchy between an original and its translation, the translated work displaces the original in a way that ensures its artistic survival: what Walter Benjamin (1923) calls its 'afterlife'. 'The translation', he writes in his essay

The Task of the Translator, 'comes after the original, of course, and in the case of important works, which never find their chosen translator at the time of their coming into being, it of course denotes the stage of the original's continued existence' (p. 31).

Just as there is no linear transmission from the parental unconscious to the child's, so too, Benjamin reminds us, a text cannot transmit its essence in any unilateral way. The 'afterlife' that resides in translation ensures the original loses its privileged status as a sovereign, autonomous work existing independently of language and time. Like the past itself, a translation is peculiarly susceptible to change; it is subject to those who come afterwards who see and read things differently. Whatever else it is then, a translation is surely not a copy. It reproduces 'not an original text, but an afterlife cloned from the (lost) life of the original' (Apter, 2006, p. 225). Its status may depend on whether we condemn it as a 'tissue of plagiarized fragments' (p. 222) – ominously, this is exactly how the children are viewed by an outside world that harvests their tissues and organs for its own medical benefit – or whether we can permit the traditional significance of originality to yield to broader considerations of the way translation can offer continued life and fresh meaning to a now obsolete original. For the children at Hailsham, these are not simply literary or academic issues; they are acute ontological predicaments. What, after all, is the meaning of a life that has lost its origins? Is there any value in a person who is merely a 'plagiarized fragment'? Interrogating these dilemmas a little further leads us to what is perhaps the most troubling question of all: is there anything unique or distinctive to be found within the child who is only a copy?

From copying to creativity

When we learn through imitation, we all become 'like' the other by borrowing certain traits, characteristics and mannerisms. These conscious and unconscious identifications, suggests Freud, are the building blocks of our identity; they inspire and instigate a revised sense of who we are. It is not simply that the ego is altered by identification; the ego is itself constituted by this partial absorption or digestion of the other into the self. Perhaps, then, it is true to say that we all clone ourselves from one another, borrowing or stealing bits and pieces in order to build a self, an ego, within. But as Kathy comes to realise, copying alone is not enough. We must be more than our identifications; we must create something new around the internal residue, the kernel of the other.

T. S. Eliot, writing about the Elizabethan playwright, Philip Massinger in 1921, argues:

> One of the surest of tests is the way in which a poet borrows. Immature poets imitate; mature poets steal; bad poets deface what they take and good poets make it into something better, or at least something different. The good poet welds his theft into a whole of feeling which is unique,

utterly different from that which it was torn; the bad poet throws it into something which has no cohesion.

(p. 114)

If all we are is our identifications, if we are only copies of each other, we miss the opportunity to make something unique and new of ourselves. As Richard Rorty (1989) points out, the realisation that one is merely a facsimile or reproduction, the Bloomian 'horror at finding oneself to be a copy or a replica' (p. 24), is to fail as a human being. Like Bloom's strong poet, Rorty argues that we need to be aware of our debt to those from whom we have stolen, those whom we imitate, but then go on creatively to 'misread' in order to rework them into something new, fresh, original. In this way, what we take in of someone – a song, a piece of writing, an analyst's words – needs to be absorbed, subsumed and remodelled. We weld our theft of otherness, as it were, into the fabric of our own subjectivity in order to create a self that is valid on its own terms.

Let us return to the missing Judy Bridgewater cassette tape. Just as Ruth is determined to find her original parent model by following her 'possible', so too Tommy is gripped by the 'possibility' that the missing tape may turn out to be the original cassette that was lost at Hailsham. But in a dizzying play on the categories of copy and original, Ishiguro offers us the fiction of a cassette tape, 'originally an LP' (p. 61), that was in turn a recording of a song by a seductive cocktail-bar singer; in other words, a replica of a copy of a recording of an event that now claims priority. Just as the 'possible' allows the children to sustain a fantasy of origins, so too the lost cassette tape constitutes a promise of authenticity. The 'fictive pretext' of an original, now sequestered within an ever-receding series of duplicates, is nonetheless what sets the children off on their quest for a story about themselves that transcends their pitiful status as disposable items bred for the convenience of the outside world.

For Tommy, finding the cassette recording may be essential to recovering a sense of the lost origins of his own life. But Kathy comes to realise that the tape's originality is not essential:

> I really appreciated having the tape – and that song – back again. Even then, it was mainly a nostalgia thing, and today, if I happen to get the tape out and look at it, it brings back memories of that afternoon in Norfolk every bit as much as it does our Hailsham days.
>
> (p. 159)

Nostalgia, of course, is not grief; it is grief's lookalike. It is not loss, but rather its pleasurably melancholic evocation. It implies a sentimental longing for, or regretful memory of, one's home or a past period of one's life. Perhaps, then, 'a nostalgia thing' is the only phrase that Kathy can deploy to convey, even to herself, the terrible losses incurred by the mimetic foundation of her existence. For the copy that is the cassette tape, itself found in a second-hand shop, evokes in her a nostalgia that might be said to mime or stand in for a grief she is unable fully to articulate. Its significance lies in the way the recorded song, the copy, acts to regenerate and recycle memories and feelings. It evokes emotional experience and in that sense is as valuable to Kathy as any original. Whether the tape is the actual one she lost at Hailsham or whether it is one of thousands of copies is irrelevant; its value lies not in its origins but rather in how it can be used to rework and add substance to her own memories and her own identity. In this way, the status of the tape can be seen to mirror the status of the children themselves. We can now understand the terrible question of their humanity, something they believe can only be secured by finding their 'possible' in the world, as secondary to their creative capacity to evoke love and desire among themselves, and to generate stories, memories and meaning from their emotional experiences.

Just as Walter Benjamin reverses the traditional priority of the original over the translation, so too does Kathy's memory ultimately prove to be more important, more durable and more meaningful than the events on which her recollections are based. At the end of the novel, she disagrees with one of the 'donors' she is caring for who claims: '[M]emories, even your most precious ones, fade surprisingly quickly. But I don't go along with that,' she argues. 'The memories I value most, I don't ever see them ever fading. I lost Ruth, then I lost Tommy, but I won't lose my memories of them' (pp. 261–2). This is no sentimental statement about how we might console ourselves after the death of a loved one. Ishiguro is rather illuminating how Kathy's ability to rework her experiences creates a sense of attachment and belonging out of the grim realities of her time at Hailsham. These original experiences have been supplanted by what we might call their 'afterlife' that now resides in her memory. It is this that ensures Kathy will 'never let go'. By continually recycling and refining her memories, she will hold on to their continued existence and survival until she, like Tommy before her, finally 'completes'.

Conclusion

Perhaps we might think of this Laplanchean ingenuity, the capacity perpetually to refashion, renew and make meaning from that which is second hand or recycled, as bearing the hallmark of what it means to be human. For Ishiguro seems to suggest that it is not the children's biological relationship to the 'possible' that secures their status as human beings, but their capacity to create or invent the 'possible' out of need and desire. It is not their artwork that establishes their souls, but their persistent attempts to weave a story about the redeeming power of art and love in their lives. It is in refashioning and redescribing their abject circumstances and curtailed futures, like Kathy's story about the singer of the song 'Never let me go, oh baby, baby, never let me go', that they repudiate their status as soulless copies and affirm the presence of a vivid inner world with a capacity for artistry and love: evidence of their ontological equivalence to 'normals' in the world.

So the informal way in which Kathy frequently addresses the reader: 'I don't know how it was where you were, but at Hailsham …' (p. 12), disguises what I see as the central, disquieting premise of the novel: that we are being addressed as peers, as fellow graduates from establishments like Hailsham who share a common frame of reference with Kathy, and who are assumed to be clones just as much as she is herself. In this way, Ishiguro is not attempting to make an ethical distinction between humans and clones by suggesting that 'we' are somehow more 'real', 'true' or 'authentic' than 'they' are; nor that he is, as the critic James Wood suggests, asking us to consider the parallels between the futility of the children's foreshortened lives and the futility of our own. Rather, I suggest he is defining our humanity precisely in terms of our kinship with clones. We are all copies of one sort or another (or copies of copies) because there was never anything original within us in the first place.

The promiscuous nature of our identifications, the contingency of our sources of selfhood are, says Oliver Sacks (2017), 'a paradoxical strength […] indifference to source allows us to assimilate what we read, what we are told, what others say and think and write and paint, as intensely and richly as if they were primary experiences' (pp. 121–2). And so concealed with the bleakness of Ishiguro's dystopian fable of the clone, we can see emerging the outlines of something more familiar and human. For although we might be indifferent to where our sources of selfhood come from, we cannot, it seems, do without the *idea* of a source itself, the notion of a constitutive basis or inner foundation on which our sense of identity is predicated. 'Men can do nothing', declares George Eliot (1876), 'without the make-believe of a beginning'. In this opening epigraph to *Daniel Deronda*, a novel that Ishiguro tangentially references in *Never Let Me Go*, Eliot draws attention to our inability to survive and thrive without a story of origins. The main protagonist of Eliot's novel suffers, like Kathy, from a state of ignorance about his ancestry; and for much of the novel, a lack of knowledge about his parentage deprives him of a secure position in the world. Only subsequently does he come to learn the truth about his Jewish heritage. Kathy's 'hazy' reading of *Daniel Deronda* at the Cottages, in which the book's 'mysterious dimension' (p. 112) is never discussed, allows the parallels between the themes in Eliot's novel and Kathy's own life to remain quietly unspoken. Nonetheless, Ishiguro positions this brief scene as the immediate backdrop to the children's trip to Norfolk, where its unassuming presence prefigures their consoling story of origins. So we might see in the myth of the 'possible' Ishiguro's artistic rendering of the self's 'make-believe of a beginning': the illusion or fiction of an essential inner core, the necessary story that provides us with a sense of uniqueness and a place in the world.

We will return to the idea of the 'make-believe of a beginning' in later chapters. Meanwhile, back in 1970s London I can still recall the intensity with which I tried to emulate the lovely, lively, singing sound of Kreisler's violin.

With the benefit of hindsight, it is easy to see that I was probably looking for an imaginary starting point, that I was using Kreisler as a musical 'possible' for myself and my dreams of becoming a violinist. Perhaps, Ishiguro intimates, our existence is formed not only via the early attachments, identifications and allegiances that have been grafted on to the psyche, but is also shaped and coloured by the various ways we respond to, reflect on and engage with artistic works. These will include the music and musicians we listen to, the books we read and the stories that most enthral, engross and involve us. These include, of course, the stories we call our own. So in psychoanalysis too, we reflect on and engage with the stories we tell about ourselves, our lives and our relationships. But if, as Stephen Grosz (2014) argues, we cannot find a way to tell our story, 'the story will eventually tell us' (p. 10), emerging in symptoms, dreams and unwanted feelings. Voicing our story allows it eventually to be rewritten, offering up another narrative 'possible', a fresh 'fictive pretext' around which we are able to dream up and experience new emotional origins: a provisional starting point, perhaps, for reworking memory, desire and subjectivity and for letting go of old stories and unwanted identifications; for crafting and re-crafting, yet again, something new within a borrowed self.

Note

1 All references in the text to *Never Let Me Go* are taken from Ishiguro, K. (2005). *Never Let Me Go*. London: Faber and Faber.

References

Apter, E. (2006). *The Translation Zone: A New Comparative Literature*. Princeton, NJ: Princeton University Press.
Aristotle (2005). *Poetics*. Cambridge, MA: Harvard University Press.
Benjamin, W. (1923). The task of the translator. In: L. Venuti (ed.), *The Translation Studies Reader*, pp. 15–25. London: Routledge, 2000.
Connolly, C. (1944). *The Unquiet Grave: A Word Cycle by Palinurus*. London: Hamish Hamilton, 1950.
Dennett, D. (1976). Conditions of personhood. In: A. Oksenberg Rorty (ed.), *The Identities of Persons*, pp. 175–196. Berkeley, CA: University of California Press. (Topics in Philosophy.)
Eliot, G. (1876). *Daniel Deronda*. London: Penguin Classics, 1995.
Eliot, T.S. (1921). *The Sacred Wood: Essays on Poetry and Criticism*. London: Faber and Faber, 1997.
Freud, S. (1918). From the history of an infantile neurosis. In: J. Strachey (ed. and trans.), *The Standard Edition of the Complete Psychological Works of Sigmund Freud*, Vol. 17, pp. 7–122. London: Hogarth.
Freud, S. (1921). Group psychology and the analysis of the ego. In: J. Strachey (ed. and trans.), *The Standard Edition of the Complete Psychological Works of Sigmund Freud*, Vol. 18, 65–144. London: Hogarth.

Freud, S. (1923). The Ego and the Id. In: J. Strachey (ed. and trans.), *The Standard Edition of the Complete Psychological Works of Sigmund Freud*, Vol. 19, pp. 1–66. London: Hogarth.
Fuss, D. (1995). *Identification Papers: Readings on Psychoanalysis, Sexuality and Culture*. London: Routledge.
Grosz, S. (2014). *The Examined Life*. London: Vintage.
Huxley, A. (1932). *Brave New World*. London: Vintage, 2007.
Ishiguro, K. (2005). *Never Let Me Go*. London: Faber and Faber.
Kermode, F. (2005). Outrageous game. *London Review of Books*, 27, 8: 21–22.
Laplanche, J. (1999). *Essays on Otherness*. London: Routledge.
Levin, I. (1976). *The Boys from Brazil*. New York: Pegasus Books.
Modell, A. (1999). The dead mother syndrome and the reconstruction of trauma. In: G. Kohon (ed.), *The Dead Mother: The Work of André Green*, pp. 76–86. London: Routledge. (The New Library of Psychoanalysis.)
Paz, O. (1971). *Translation: Literature and Letters*, trans. Irene del Corral (*Traduccion: Literatura y Literalidad*). Barcelona: Tusquets.
Rorty, R. (1989). *Contingency, Irony, and Solidarity*. Cambridge: Cambridge University Press.
Sacks, O. (2017). The fallibility of memory. In: *The River of Consciousness*. London: Picador.
Toffler, I. (1970). *Future Shock*. London: Bantam, 1990.
Winnicott, D.W. (1960). Ego distortion in terms of true and false self. In: *The Maturational Processes and the Facilitating Environment*, pp. 140–152. London: Karnac, 1990.

Chapter 2

The wager of faith in fiction and psychoanalysis
Colm Tóibín's *The Testament of Mary*

> Faith makes us, and not we it; and faith makes its own forms.
> (Ralph Waldo Emerson, 1850, p. 101)

Introduction

Climbing the north staircase to the friars' cells in the fifteenth-century Dominican convent of San Marco in Florence, what seems at first to be a distant cloud of Mediterranean pinks, sepias and lustrous gold only gradually comes into focus. It is a scene at once familiar and extraordinary. The Annunciation, painted by Fra Angelico in 1450, is carefully positioned at the top of the stairs, inviting us to pause for a moment before the life-sized image depicting the Archangel Gabriel visiting the Virgin Mary to tell her that she is about to conceive the Son of God. Mary, dressed in her customary blue, is sitting modestly on a simple, wooden stool in a cloister with her hands crossed over her breast. Her head is bending reverently towards her radiant visitor whose magnificent, gleaming, multicolour wings announce his celestial status as emissary from God. Mary seems surprisingly calm and serene. Her gaze, focused on Gabriel's eyes, gives little hint of surprise at being the recipient of such unexpected news. However, we might choose to see in the slight inclination of her body towards the angel, as if she is listening to words she cannot quite believe, a moment of hesitation as the full realisation of her divine duty becomes borne upon her. Of course, we already know from St Luke that Mary chose to accept her role as Mother of the Son of God, responding to the angel in the beautiful words of the Gospel: 'Behold the handmaid of the Lord. May it be done unto me according to thy Word'.

The frescoes at San Marco have been studied extensively by art historians, with numerous scholarly works (e.g. Hood, 1993; Lloyd and White, 1998) documenting the power, subtlety and influence of Fra Angelico's artistic and religious imagination. But by the time he was commissioned by Cosimo de' Medici to decorate the newly established convent of San Marco, Fra Angelico had already painted two different versions of the Annunciation. As Hodge

DOI: 10.4324/9781003325468-3

(2006) points out, this particular fresco unusually lacks many of the symbols that were traditionally used to suggest the sanctity of the Virgin Mary. There are no white lilies to convey her virginity, nor does Gabriel appear to be interrupting her reading of the scriptures, a common artistic device used to index Mary's piety. Indeed, unlike his previous, more elaborate and colourful paintings of the same scene, Fra Angelico seems to have made a deliberate decision to keep this version of the Annunciation as simple and spare as possible. We do not know the reason for this, but given the fresco's central position in the convent, we might imagine that he wanted to allow his fellow friars maximum creative freedom to fill in the details themselves of what would have been a very familiar story; to use the simplicity of the fresco as artistic inspiration for prayer, meditation and the practice of their faith.

There can be few scenes from the Bible more frequently represented within Christian iconography than the Annunciation. That so many versions of Mary have appeared over the centuries is testament not only to the imaginative appeal that she holds as Theotokos, or God-bearer, but also to the dearth of information we have about the life of this teenage mother from Nazareth. Of course, biography was not the concern of New Testament writers, who were interested simply in demonstrating the fulfilment of Old Testament prophecies. Nonetheless, as Warner (2000) points out, the absence of details about Mary's life in the bible is a lacuna that has come to be filled with an accretion of myths and stories that makes her a figure 'that has been formed and animated by different people for different reasons and is truly a popular creation' (p. xxiv). All we do know, according to Christian theology and the work of artists such as Fra Angelico, is that there was a primal scene symbolised by her encounter with the angel where Mary was asked to make a choice. Faced with the angel and filled with doubt – St Luke tells us that Mary was 'perplexed' by the angel's words – she nonetheless assents to her sacred duty: 'may it be done unto me'. It is a courageous act of faith, in which she commits herself to the Holy Spirit and thereby becomes receptacle of the divine. Richard Kearney (2010) calls this decisive instant the 'wager of faith': a critical moment where we respond to the Stranger with either hospitality or hostility, where we accept or refuse the advent of the sacred. It is the inaugural encounter with the other that sponsors the choice of faith.

It is to this moment of wager that Colm Tóibín's (2013) provocatively titled *The Testament of Mary* returns us. In this brief, lyrical novella, also staged as a play, Tóibín offers a moving first-person account of the grieving Mary's life in exile in Ephesus, twenty years after the crucifixion of her son. However, this newly imagined voice of Mary has been seen by some as shocking, with both book and play deemed to be a blasphemous reworking of a sacred truth. The play's opening on Broadway was marked by Catholic demonstrations denouncing it as 'not only blasphemous but heretical. It presents a caricature of the Blessed Virgin Mary and implicitly denies all of the dogmas the Church has defined in her regard' (*Los Angeles Times*, March 2013).

Fictional reworkings of texts deemed to be sacred are scarcely new. They rarely receive unanimous praise and on occasions have been known to provoke violence. One of the best known predecessors of Tóibín's *The Testament of Mary*, Salman Rushdie's (1988) *The Satanic Verses*, resulted in the Ayatollah Khomeini's fatwa in which he called on Muslims worldwide to kill Rushdie and his publishers. Philip Pullman's (1995) more recent trilogy *His Dark Materials*, too, was roundly condemned by the powerful US-based Catholic League which campaigned successfully against the film version *The Golden Compass*, declaring it promoted atheism. Against this backdrop of wounded belief systems and book-burning outrage, it would be all too easy to read Tóibín's novella simply as a kind of anti-Catholic political thriller in which a young rebel is transformed into a god via a band of misfit friends, hysterical fans and susceptible followers. I think this would be to miss the point of what is an artful and intensely thought-provoking book. For by inviting the reader to believe his fictional account of Mary's life alongside an imaginative reconstruction of how her role as Mother of Jesus came to be written, I think Tóibín sets out to achieve two crucial and interrelated aims: first, to call the authority of texts normally held as sacred into question; and second, to thereby open up a space in which our traditional credos can be reconstituted or salvaged in the light of imagined alternatives.

The power of Tóibín's tale rests on his ability to create and sustain this fictive space in which a wager of faith becomes a vivid reality for the reader and constitutes the fulcrum on which the entire novella turns. In his reimagining of a Mary who stubbornly refuses to believe that her son is the Son of God, Tóibín raises questions about the basis on which we have come to be inhabited by the story of that inner presence of otherness deemed to be divine. However, the reception of the other whose inner presence is constitutive of subjectivity, if not divinity, is equally a central preoccupation for psychoanalysis. In this chapter, then, I want to draw on Tóibín's story as a means of investigating how we understand the notion of faith in psychoanalytic theory and practice. But by setting out my thesis in this way, I must first recognise that the relationship between faith and psychoanalysis is almost as troubled as the relationship that exists between literature and psychoanalysis and may in fact have much in common with it. For just as psychoanalysis has traditionally attempted to exert authority over the field of literature through its claim to explanatory power, so too has psychoanalysis chosen in the past to claim priority over religion by emphasising its defensive function within the psyche. In *The Future of an Illusion*, Freud (1927) claimed that all aspects of religious life were 'illusions, fulfilments of the oldest, strongest and most urgent wishes of mankind' (p. 30) and that giving up our infantile need for the protection of an all-powerful father was the mark of emotional maturity. But if, as Rieff (1966) points out, 'Freud has systemised our unbelief' (p. 40), it is scarcely surprising that the concept of faith has since struggled to find a foothold within psychoanalytic theory, despite Bion's (1970) call for analysts to approach their work in a state of 'faith that there is an ultimate reality and truth' (p. 31). More recently, however, there seems to have been what Starr (2008) calls a 'gradual rapprochement' between the two fields of study, where a cultural shift away from compliance with traditional religious doctrine towards respect for the individual's own inner spiritual orientation has allowed both religion and psychoanalysis to acknowledge the role faith may play in psychic change and transformation. Contemporary psychoanalysts such as Eigen (1999), Ghent (1999), Neri (2005), Safran (1999, 2006), Sorenson (2004) and Spezzano and Gargiulo (2013), among others, have integrated their theological interests with psychoanalytic theory alongside religious scholars such as Ostow (1995) and Zornberg (1995, 2002), who have drawn from psychoanalysis in their understanding of religious belief.

I am not able, nor am I qualified, to approach my topic from the perspective of theological scholarship; nor indeed can I claim any expertise in the history of art. Nonetheless, my aim in this chapter rests on a willingness to cross disciplinary divides in order to bring imaginative ideas from the domains of fiction and postmodern theology within the purview of existing psychoanalytic thinking. Such cross-fertilisation carries certain risks, yet I believe offers the potential for fresh insights and different ways of thinking that can refresh ideas and concepts that have become familiar over time. More specifically, I will use the illusory space of fiction that Tóibín opens up in *The Testament of Mary* as a provocative spur to understanding the way in which faith may be conceived of as wager within both fiction and psychoanalysis. Developing my topic via Kearney's (2010) notion of anatheism as well as through a discussion of hospitality and alterity, I will briefly draw on Winnicott's (1971) paper 'The use of an object' to illustrate the existential nature of the psychoanalytic wager of faith. As we shall see, this takes us into a consideration of the significance of testimony within psychoanalytic work.

The Testament of Mary[1]

Tóibín sets his story within a story, situating Mary as necessary participant in as well as critical witness to the creation of a narrative that was to become central to Christian identity: the life and suffering of her son Jesus. We first meet Mary when she is living in exile in Ephesus, 20 years after the violent death of her son. Now an elderly woman, traumatised by what she has seen and wracked by painful memories, she is tortured by her failure to save Jesus from his fate. Mary is guarded by two disciples of Jesus who are engaged in the onerous task of writing down a record of what happened to her son. They continually question her about the events leading up to the crucifixion, but she refuses to co-operate with the story they so clearly want to hear. For while Mary cannot read or write, she is all too aware that what is being written is a version of events that she does not recognise:

> I have asked him to read the words aloud to me but he will not. I know that he has written of things that neither he saw nor I saw. I know that he has also given shape to what I lived through and he witnessed, and that he has made sure that these words will matter, that they will be listened to.
>
> (p. 5)

From the outset then, Tóibín's novella is purposely framed as a vindication of Mary's own testimony, offered in direct contrast to the words that will later become the basis of the New Testament. Tóibín imagines Mary's story via a staging of three central events in the Gospels: the raising of Lazarus from the dead, the wedding at Cana where Jesus changes water into wine, and the final scenes at Calvary culminating in Jesus's crucifixion. In St John's Gospel, the miracle of the raising of Lazarus is presented at length and in detail as the final and most important sign that Jesus gives; it is this event that leads directly to the decision of Caiaphas and the Sanhedrin to kill Jesus. But in Tóibín's reworking of the Gospel, the raising of Lazarus is placed much earlier in the story and is framed as an event that Mary neither witnesses nor condones. Instead, she is deeply disturbed by the notion of bringing someone back from the dead: 'no-one should tamper with the fullness that is death' (p. 31). Indeed, the description of the dead Lazarus being called back into life is presented not as miraculous but rather as a truly chilling event:

> the figure dirtied with clay and covered with graveclothes wound around him began with great uncertainty to move [...] It was as though the earth beneath him was pushing him and then letting him be still [...] like some strange new creature jerking and wriggling towards life.
>
> (p. 35)

Tóibín subsequently places Lazarus alongside Mary and Jesus at the wedding feast in Cana. The excitement of the guests at what has happened to Lazarus together with Jesus's presence means that Mary and her son are now both in danger of being killed by the authorities. She tries to persuade Jesus to leave the wedding, but finds to her dismay that he ignores her: 'he had begun to talk to others, high-flown talk and riddles, using strange proud terms to describe himself and his task in the world [...] I heard him saying that he was the Son of God' (p. 47). Realising that she will not be able to save Jesus, Mary slips away from the wedding party and returns to Nazareth. The political unease at Jesus's actions now takes on a more menacing quality and shortly after her return, Mary learns that her son has been taken by the Sanhedrin and is to be crucified. She reluctantly agrees to go to Jerusalem for her own safety and, hopeful of seeing Jesus, disguises herself to accompany the crowd to the crucifixion.

It is here that Tóibín is utterly unsparing in his detailed portrayal of a scene filled with horror, cruelty and blood. This Jesus doesn't suffer quietly or easily. He fights back; he screams with pain and writhes in agony as he is nailed to the cross. Mary forces herself to stay and watch the dreadful, drawn-out suffering of her son, steeling herself to be with him at the moment of his death. But in a startling reworking of the familiar Christian iconography of the *Stabat Mater*, Tóibín refuses to offer us any consolation. For here there is no grieving mother at the foot of the cross, no *Pietà* holding Christ's dead, mutilated body across her knees, no *Mater Dolorosa*. Tóibín's Mary, in the midst of trauma, grief and terror, nonetheless realises with great clarity that her own life is in imminent danger; and to save herself, she slips away to safety before Jesus dies. Twenty years on, still brimming with guilt and remorse, she finally chokes out the frightful words that she has held back for so long: 'For years I have comforted myself with the thought of how long I remained there [...] But I must say it once, I must let the words out [...] I would leave him to die alone if I had to. And that is what I did' (p. 84).

Following the crucifixion, and on the run with her guardian and Lazarus's sister, Mary and her companion both dream of Jesus rising up from the earth along with water overflowing from a well. The dream is so powerful that Mary feels it acquires an almost tangible quality: 'what happened in our dreams took on more flesh, had more substance, than our lives when we were conscious, alert, aware' (p. 93). Indeed, it is this very tangibility – a measure of Mary's own desperate desire for her son to return from the dead – that is subsequently written into biblical history by disciples who intend to make Jesus's resurrection the linchpin of their new Christian theology.

Mary remains consumed with guilt for the rest of her life. She is constantly badgered by her guardians to tell again the details of what happened, to add further nuances that will flesh out the story they want to hear, the story that she knows is not true. She protests that 'I never saw his grave, I never washed his body' (p. 101). But Mary's testament is met with determined opposition, if not outright contradiction: '"You were there," my guide said. "You held his body when it was taken down from the cross". His companion nodded' (p. 101).

As readers we know that, as Mother of Sorrows, Mary will be portrayed by artists for millennia to come at the foot of the cross, weeping over the body of her dead son. But in Tóibín's version, Mary's sorrow is a private grief, born of a sense of personal guilt that not only did she fail to protect her son from a humiliating and protracted death, but that she failed to stay with him to the end.

By the end of the book, we find Tóibín's Mary living out her days fearing that the men who are guarding her are the ones who will 'thrive and prevail' long after she is gone. She has refused to believe in the new story being constructed around the life and death of her son, a story written by men that will form the basis of the new Christian religion stretching across the world. Instead, she takes solace in a much older story still active in Ephesus: the maternal cult of Artemis, the many-breasted Greek virgin goddess of mythology.

Faith and fiction: Kearney's 'anatheism'

I have wanted to offer this brief summary of Tóibín's story as a way of conveying the extent to which his novella is startling, even shocking, in its portrayal of Mary, not as Mother of God, but rather as subject in her own right. 'New Testament figures', claims Oppenheimer (2012), 'do not really have interior lives. They are mythical types'. While the traditional version of Mary allows us only to think of her in her capacity as receptacle of the divine, Tóibín deliberately sets out to unsettle, disconcert and surprise us into thinking about Mary as a person, as a subject, as a woman. For those whose religious faith rests on the text that Tóibín so powerfully reimagines, it is challenging, even perturbing, to read.

But Tóibín is not, of course, the only writer to make the radical attempt to rework our relationship to the God of traditional theology, and it could be argued that his work emerges from a contemporary and postmodern cultural recasting of 'strong' metaphysical dogma. Derrida's (1995) 'religion without religion', Caputo's (2006) notion of 'weak theology' and Kearney's (2001) return to a 'God who may be' are all concerned with subjecting the abstract, sacred, eternal, powerful God of traditional theology to doubt, reinterpretation, subjectivity and secularity. Kearney's notion of anatheism, a 'return to God after God', expresses a way of relating to the sacred in the aftermath of the social, cultural and intellectual 'death of God' announced by Nietzsche, Marx and Freud. As a philosophical response to our contemporary disillusionment with religion and the widespread desacralising of the world, Kearney (2010) differentiates anatheism from dogmatic theism as well as militant atheism, refusing any absolutist positions either for or against the divine. Anatheism, proposes Kearney (2015), constitutes 'a radical opening to someone or something that was lost and forgotten by Western metaphysics ... and needs to be recalled again' (p. 9). 'The *ana*', he writes,

> signals a movement of return to what I call a primordial wager,to an inaugural instant of reckoning at the root of belief. It marks a reopening of that space where we are free to choose between faith and nonfaith. As such, anatheism is about the option of retrieved belief. [...] Anatheism, in short, is an invitation to revisit what might be termed a primary scene of religion; the encounter with a radical Stranger who we choose, or don't choose, to call God.
>
> (p. 7)

Kearney argues that one of the most potent ways of returning us to the moment of anatheistic wager is via the work of poets, writers and artists: those whose dramatic readings and interpretations allow us to enter imaginatively into the lives of people and events portrayed in biblical or other sacred texts and which offer the possibility of a return to the sacred moment of choice. The attempt to reposition faith in the light of our disenchantment with religious dogma and ideology is clearly part of Tóibín's artistic project in *The Testament of Mary*. His re-visioning of Mary's life distances us from our traditional beliefs while at the same time offering us the potential for faith of a different order. Fiction's capacity to bring into being imagined worlds is, of course, profoundly counterfactual. To read fictional literature is to believe, albeit provisionally, in the existence of characters and situations that we know don't exist. In Tóibín's story, we are asked to believe in the possible existence of his version of Mary and her account of events. While we are taken through her story, we believe 'as if' she existed in just the same way 'as' believers endorse the canonical account of her life in the Bible. It is by juxtaposing his hypothetical account of Mary's life with the familiar account that he knows his readers hold that Tóibín not only offers us a Mary who wrestles with the putative divinity of her son; he also allows us, while we read, to defer questions of belief and unbelief and identify with his version of Mary 'as if it were true. We have been given poetic licence to suspend traditional religious belief, and accept 'in good faith' the very different version of events with which we are presented and which allows us to imagine otherwise.

But by blurring the distinction between faith and fiction Tóibín also allows us to read Mary's story 'as if' it were the Bible. Of course, the mimetic function of fiction releases possible worlds of belief and action that differ substantially from the claims to authority and universality made by the Bible. Stories from scripture cannot be read simply for the purposes of entertainment or make-believe; they point to an inner secret or hidden meaning which is conveyed, in part at least, by the very particular language deployed. Auerbach's (1953) distinction between classical literature and the Bible points out that biblical language is deliberately brief and sparse, concerned with conveying only the decisive elements of a sacred narrative without the addition of superfluous detail. It is, as the King James Version of the Bible perhaps best demonstrates, language at its most sublime and majestic: language making a claim to ultimate authority and truth. By contrast, Tóibín's Mary tells her story in language that is simple, rhythmic and repetitive: language that is very different from the one being prepared for the Gospel account of events. Let us recall that Tóibín's Mary is illiterate. Her words are not freighted with a background of concealed, sacred significance requiring authoritative theological interpretation. Rather, she uses words that are colloquial, informal, ordinary, maternal. Yet by offering the first-person perspective of someone commenting on events privileged by sacred texts, Tóibín ensures that Mary's fictive testimony competes with the testimony of the Bible to claim a similarly compelling authority.

But if the fictive 'as if' enables us to read Mary's version of events 'as if' it were the Bible, it also enables us to think of the Bible 'as if' it were fiction: 'as if' imaginative story rather than 'as' sacred text. Just as Fra Angelico's artistic vision of the Annunciation gave his fellow monks imaginative free rein to fill in the details of the story, so too Tóibín's story points to the necessary role of the imagination in all religious belief. Certainly, it could be argued that without imaginative reinterpretations, the meaning of canonical texts becomes fixed or static, losing the vitality and immediacy required if they are to speak freshly to new groups and generations. This interpretative or fictive element in faith is located by Kearney (2010) in the cultural shift from ancient religious rites to their symbolic representation in the Greek tragedies. In these great early dramas, religious or sacrificial rituals were transmuted into powerful narratives during which the audience suspended their literal belief in the gods and heroes in favour of something figural or metaphorical. Such mimetic re-creation aimed at opening up a gap, a breach, between events and their dramatic retelling that not only ensured a certain distance or perspective from which to view the unfolding characters and situation, but also ensured empathy with those whose suffering was portrayed in the drama. Kearney suggests that the gap opened up by the fictional rendering of events transports us to the future anterior, to the undecidable space of what might have been. It is here, gripped by a story that demands emotional as well as spiritual engagement, that we are returned to the originary moment of wager where faith is once again a choice.

It is surely no coincidence that Tóibín himself has described how his idea for *The Testament of Mary* had its basis in an imagined visit by the disciple John to the theatre in Ephesus. He suggests that John was struggling to write his Gospel and wanted to find the most powerful way of conveying the events surrounding Jesus's crucifixion and death. The theatre, Tóibín suggests, was showing a play by Aeschylus and it was this, he argues, that caught John's imagination:

> and then what he saw in the theatre lifted him out of his dilemma. His imagination soared with the crowd around him as, in some play that has been lost to us, he watched the enactment of a grieving woman imploring, crying out, and gaining power from her own voice. And then he watched someone seeming to return from the dead. The effect on the crowd around him and on himself was tremendous. Thus he found out what to do when he began to write his Gospel ... He began to see the influence his writing might have.
>
> (2014b)

This is, I think, an astonishing piece of imagination – or rather, of imagined imagination – where Tóibín speculates that the inspiration for John's account of the crucifixion and his reasons for deciding to place Mary at the foot of the cross might have been inspired by watching a play, a Greek tragedy; and that the Gospel of St. John, soon to become the cornerstone of the new Christian religion, could itself have derived from a piece of dramatic fiction. Rather than merely hollowing out religious texts in favour of an empty secularism, then, I see Tóibín's *The Testament of Mary* demonstrating how we as readers and believers come to have faith in the power of story, and how stories inhabit us and become woven into the fabric of our lives. By retelling and reimagining Mary's story, Tóibín shows how the creative space of fiction can work to break these old stories open, acting as the cornerstone of a second faith that is different from our first, 'naïve' faith: one that allows us the freedom to imagine otherwise, to tell another story – the story of how things might have been.

The wager of faith in psychoanalysis

What can we as clinicians learn from Tóibín's artistic re-visioning of the Gospel? What are the implications of the wager of faith in fiction for how we might understand any notion of faith in psychoanalysis? Indeed, how might we understand 'faith' in the first place? In order to sharpen the contours of these complex questions, we might do well to start with Treanor's (2010) discussion of Kearney's anatheism in which he attempts to distinguish between faith, belief and knowledge. To know something, he suggests, requires evidence or credentials that establish our knowledge as 'true', while to believe something is to accept it without the need for any such verification. Faith, however, is different. It is a particular type of belief that includes a readiness to commit, to act. It is a wager on which everything is staked.

'The distinction between belief and knowledge is epistemic', he writes,

> and has to do with how certain we are about a given proposition, while the difference between belief and faith is existential [...] having to do with our commitment to live in the light of a certain proposition.
>
> (p. 549)

In this sense, as Treanor argues, faith may be considered different from knowledge in terms of what it is possible to verify, whereas faith may be considered different from belief in terms of what we are prepared to do: the extent to which we are committed, willing and able to take a 'leap of faith' that could change our lives.

While it may be difficult to sustain Treanor's separation of the epistemological and the existential aspects of faith – they are surely two sides of the same anatheistic wager – the distinction may be a useful starting point for our discussion. Kearney (2010) seems particularly sympathetic to a faith that is characterised by a wholehearted, imaginative and engaged orientation, not simply one that relies on proof or evidence. His notion of anatheism is primarily concerned with articulating a faith that rests more on transformation than on calculation. Tóibín, too, in his reworking of Mary's life, points us towards the transformative potential of literature, where the fictive 'as if' of poetic licence vividly engages the reader in an existential rather than epistemological wager of faith. Taking Fra Angelico's painting of the Annunciation as analogy, we might imagine Tóibín's artistic message to be the beating of wings at the door heralding the arrival of the angel Gabriel, and the annunciatory potential of the creative work as awaiting entrance in the form of assent from an individual willing to hear what it might have to say.

The existential wager here pre-eminently rests on the stance we take up in the presence of the creative work of art, the spirit in which we respond to the provocation of its message. The issue of reception is central. Is the message something to be accepted and welcomed, or refused and repudiated? There seems to be a link here, as Kearney (2010) notes, with ancient notions of hospitality. To offer hospitality to the Stranger is always to encounter the unfamiliar and to welcome what is new and different into our home. But hospitality does not only refer to concrete interactions with those we do not know. It refers, in metaphorical form, to a kind of attentiveness to 'otherness' that includes a receptivity to that which is mystical or holy: an openness to what is most unfamiliar or 'foreign' within ourselves and to those with whom we come into relationship. For this reason, as Levinas (1969) intimates, the figure of the Stranger is always to be considered sacred by virtue of embodying something 'other', something different, something in excess of what we can contain within ourselves. In his etymological analysis, Benveniste (1969) points out that the term hospitality is derived from the Latin root *hostis*, which carries the dual meaning of host as well as stranger or enemy. The host is the one who agrees to lay down his or her weapons, welcoming the Stranger into a mutual relationship of trust. But in Derrida's (2000) reading of Benveniste, hospitality is also linked to a second, related term *hospes*, which contains within it the root word *pot*, meaning master, from which we get *potestas* or power. Hospitality, then, contains within it the notion of power, where the host has the authority to welcome – or refuse – foreigners or strangers into the home. Hospitality is thus a term of considerable tension and ambiguity. It is never a given, never guaranteed, and our response to the Stranger, our willingness to grant him or her admission to our home, ultimately entails an existential wager of faith: that the other will turn out to be someone to whom we might want to listen, who is worth receiving, rather than someone who is merely exploitative, greedy or murderous.

The literary critic George Steiner (1989) argues for just such a spirit of hospitality when we are confronted with the message of writers and artists who try to give otherness creative form. Our attitude towards the work of art, he suggests, requires a kind of inner receptiveness or openness that I take to be constitutive of Kearney's inaugural encounter: a rendezvous with alterity in which we do not read the novel so much as encounter it, in which we do not look at the painting so much as relate to it, and in which we do not listen to the song so much as feel it in our bones. Receiving the work of art in this way, I think, entails accepting its message 'in good faith', the kind of faith that is prior to any knowledge or calculation. It speaks of a relationship that St Anselm characterises as *fides quaerens intellectum*, or 'faith seeking knowledge'. It is akin to Derrida's (2000) notion of 'absolute hospitality', in which love of the host for the guest precedes and surpasses whatever we may come to know of him or her. Derrida's (2000) messianic hospitality, a hospitality that is always 'to come',

> requires that I open up my home and that I give not only to the foreigner, but to the absolute, unknown, anonymous other, and that I give place to them, that I let them come, that I let them arrive, and take place in the place I offer them, without asking of them either reciprocity (entering into a pact) or even their names.
>
> (p. 24)

In relation to the novel, the painting or the song, such hospitality is constituted by an existential moment of choice requiring a cordial open-mindedness, a generous willingness to hear and engage with what the artist has to say in much the same way as we would be willing to hear the words of the Stranger we have invited into our home. Of course, not all strangers turn out to be divine. Literary, artistic or musical works are not all of equal worth, nor are they all equally accessible. Some may be formulated in ways that are remote or abstruse, and hospitality to the artist's message may yet prove ill-founded if it turns out to be unintelligible or unrealisable. Disappointment and disillusion are necessary risks we must take, for 'without the gamble on welcome', says Steiner (1989), 'no door can be opened when freedom knocks' (p. 156).

Perhaps these ideas about our reception of the artistic message can help us to think freshly about the reception of alterity within psychoanalysis. For when we read Tóibín's story, just as when we see or listen to what the artist or composer has to say, '[w]e seek to make out' as Steiner (1989) says, 'the intelligibility, the claims upon us of his gestures and discourse. We realise full well that our comprehension, even as it deepens into intimacy, most particularly where it deepens into intimacy, will remain partial, fragmentary, subject to error and to revaluation' (p. 176). The excess, the surplus, the sheer otherness that inheres within the novel or work of art finds its correlate in the alterity of the other whom we encounter within psychoanalysis, an otherness that will always exceed our capacity to know or penetrate its enigmatic core. In both cases, hospitality towards the other requires a conjectural, provisional sensibility that maintains a certain 'negative capability' entailing a praxis of expectant waiting: a 'gamble on welcome', as Steiner (1989) says, that precludes any rush to conviction or certainty.

There is surprisingly little in the psychoanalytic literature that specifically addresses this 'gamble on welcome'. A notable exception is Lacan's (2006a, 2006b) extended discussion of Pascal's wager on the existence of God that is provided in Seminars XIII and XVI. Bearing in mind Treanor's (2010) distinction between the epistemological and existential aspects of faith, however, I see Lacan's deployment of Pascal principally as a means of indexing a calculative, epistemological wager based on what we can or cannot know of the symbolic 'Other'. Here, I prefer to follow Kearney in privileging the existential issue of what we *do* in the face of alterity, our willingness to engage wholeheartedly with otherness. Writers such as Eigen (1999), for example, understand the patient's faith as a quest for emotional intensity and authenticity within the psychoanalytic relationship: 'a way of experiencing that is undertaken with one's whole being, all out, "with all one's heart, with all one's soul, and with all one's might"' (p. 3). These qualities of passion and commitment are also discussed by Ghent (1999), who seeks to develop an understanding of the role of emotional surrender in promoting a radical transformation of the self.

The existential wager within psychoanalysis is perhaps best characterised in Winnicott's (1971) seminal paper 'The Use of an Object'. It is exceptionally difficult, of course, to do justice to the richness and density of Winnicott's thinking in any brief summary. But reading his paper in the light of *The Testament of Mary* may help to clarify the aleatory nature of faith I am trying to elucidate here. For just as Tóibín returns his readers to a vivid, fictive space in which the choice of faith is once again a reality, so too, suggests Winnicott, is the patient in psychoanalysis returned to an illusory space of transitional experiencing in which there is an inaugural encounter with otherness. It is within this liminal area of transitional space that Winnicott outlines developmental processes that allow the infant to distinguish between what is 'me' and what is 'not me'. This psychic recalibration enables an awareness of the other beyond the infant's omnipotent control. Crucially, however, otherness is never assured. It subsists not in demonstrable certainties, but rather in what I am calling here an existential, lived wager that its presence can and will be maintained despite the risk of its liability to loss and change.

In his well-known discussion of the shift from object-relating to object-usage, Winnicott (1971) points out:

> This thing that there is in between relating and use is the subject's placing of the object outside the area of the subject's omnipotent control; that is, the subject's perception of the object as an external phenomenon, not a projective entity, in fact recognition of it as an entity in its own right.
>
> (p. 105)

Discussing the astonishingly delicate and complex psychic negotiation that Winnicott goes on to imagine would take me far beyond the scope of this chapter. What is significant here, however, is that the object's very alterity sponsors destructive attacks in which we might say the subject wagers all on the existence and surviving presence of the other. The stakes are high, for 'the experience depends', warns Winnicott bleakly, 'on the object's capacity to survive' (p. 107). There is always the risk that the object may simply collapse, degrade or become useless, failing to break free of the subject's omnipotent projective mechanisms. In this encounter with otherness, where the subject is gambling everything on 'finding externality itself' (p. 107), there can be no foregone conclusion, no certain outcome. Hospitality operates here on the very knife-edge of hostility. Ghent (1999) vividly describes the phenomenology of the infant's lived experience in the following terms:

> One might imagine the subject saying to the object, 'I went all out, completely vulnerable, in the faith that someone was out there – and it turned out to be true, as I could only have known by destroying you with all my might and yet here you are. I love you.
>
> (p. 214)

I want to suggest that the full-blooded, 'all out' quality of commitment highlighted by Ghent indexes a faith in alterity that lies prior to any knowledge or understanding. Indeed, in 'creating' the object through destructive attack, the baby inaugurates, in fantasy, the very existence of an otherness which only later, and with some difficulty, it may come partially to know. We might say, going back to St Anselm, that the baby's 'all out' love is a form of 'faith seeking knowledge'. It constitutes what I take to be the central psychoanalytic wager of faith in alterity itself: an existential – not calculative – wager that must be lived and repeated many times over before the resilience and survival of otherness can be felt, trusted and known.

In such a brief outline, I have inevitably glossed over many subtleties in Winnicott's thinking that bear much deeper discussion. Nonetheless, I hope the schematic framework outlined here is sufficient to index at least some of the psychic coordinates at play within the psychoanalytic wager of faith. Perhaps it also serves to illuminate an issue with more weighty implications: how survival of the object can be thought of as symbolic of the survival of that inner presence of alterity many mystical traditions see as the basis of faith. Psychoanalysis has traditionally fought shy of such claims, preferring to assign our experience of alterity firmly to the unconscious.[2] Yet if we imagine, along with Winnicott, that our early, illusory experiences within transitional space lie at the heart of our adult capacity to enjoy and make use of the fictive 'as if' space within literature, drama, art and music, then we might also imagine these developmental experiences as paving a psychic path to our adult search for the sacred, however we conceive it. Recall that Winnicott (1971) regards the potential space between mother and baby 'as sacred to the individual' (p. 121). It is possible, then, that our capacity to 'imagine otherwise' – a capacity to which Tóibín himself so richly attests – constitutes an umbilical cord linking us to the dimension of transcendence: to an originary experience of alterity or otherness that is more than we can ever encompass. In saying this, I do not mean to return us to religious faith any more than I think Tóibín does, though that is, of course, one of the choices open to us at the moment of wager. Rather, I suggest that religious faith may be woven from the same psychic yarn as the one spun early on in life: one that knits otherness so tightly within the self that it takes up residence as an inner unseen guest in whose presence we may come to have the capacity, as Winnicott later suggests, to be alone.

Testimony: the psychoanalytic wager

The capacity to be alone, to bear solitude, is the necessary precondition for the act of testifying or bearing witness to one's truth. Felman (1992) writes: 'To bear witness is to bear the solitude of a responsibility and to bear the responsibility, precisely, of that solitude' (p. 3). Tóibín's Mary is testifying to what she herself has seen and heard and it is determined, despite the pressure from her guardians, that she will not give false witness: 'Just as I cannot breathe the breath of another or help the heart of someone else to beat [...] I cannot say more than I can say' (p. 4). By taking responsibility for speaking her truth, a truth that she and she alone can speak, Mary is placed in a uniquely precarious situation.

But so too is the patient in psychoanalysis. In offering an account of his or her life to the analyst who listens, the patient is, like Mary, in the unique situation of bearing witness to his or her own story. Yet just as we cannot know the 'truth' of Tóibín's version of Mary's life, so too we cannot know the 'truth' of our own. For if, as Freud (1923) suggests, our subjectivity is constituted by the presence of the other within, if the introduction of alterity into the ego precedes the formation of a self that may, one day, come to bear witness to its own personal truth, then any story that we subsequently come to tell about our lives is necessarily incomplete, estranged from itself from the outset. Indeed, psychoanalysis is predicated on the presence of an unconscious that alienates us from the conditions of our emergence as subjects. We are 'fearfully and wonderfully made', sings the psalmist in the King James Bible; we are shaped in ways we cannot know by the other who becomes the basis of a self and an unconscious we call our own but of which we are radically dispossessed. In this sense, the patient in psychoanalysis is asked to bear the responsibility of being witness to a truth that can never be owned, a truth to which he or she must constantly testify yet which is forever unavailable. 'My account of myself', writes Butler (2005), 'is partial, haunted by that for which I can devise no definitive story' (p. 40). And yet, as Tóibín's imaginative retelling of Mary's life shows, the undecidability of our account, its radical unknowability, does not necessarily refute the validity of any story we narrate, though it may offer the potential for breaking it open. Its very undecidability is what opens up a fictive space that allows us the freedom to imagine the story otherwise and permits faith in the possibility of a different life – a different story – to thereby emerge. It is this space that returns us to the inaugural moment of choice where we are able to choose this story rather than another to be the one we allow to inhabit and nourish us. Perhaps this is precisely the 'gamble on welcome', the existential wager of faith we must risk if we are to undertake a psychoanalysis.

By way of concluding, let us return to the end of Tóibín's story. We find Mary back at home in Ephesus, listening to her guardians who are once again attempting to explain to her the importance of what has happened, of how her son will change the world. But now they insist on telling her about the circumstances of Jesus's conception, a story that we as readers know will become the celebrated biblical version of the Annunciation, the one so vividly imagined – and reimagined – by Fra Angelico and thousands of artists after him. But Mary will not listen:

> I know what happened. I know that my own happiness in those first months when I was with child felt strange and special, that I lived in way that was different [...] Later, I learned that this is how we all prepare ourselves to give birth and to nurture, that it comes from the body itself and makes its way into the spirit and it does not seem ordinary.
> (pp. 99–100)

Mary's faith, we learn by the end of this remarkable book, lies not in the new God of Christianity, nor in any suggestion that her son Jesus was the Son of God. Her faith is the faith of a mother who believes only in what she remembers of her child. And so, instead of converting to the story being created by the disciples about Jesus's divinity, Mary's faith rests on the story she continues to tell herself about the human relationship she had with her son. Rather than believing in the inner, unseen presence of a deity, Mary movingly recalls the inner, unseen presence of her unborn child, a physical presence that she remembers 'felt strange and special' (p. 99). The ordinary, yet extraordinary, presence of otherness within is seamlessly transferred by Tóibín from the domain of the divine to the domain of the secular, where the simple story of a baby growing within the womb of its mother is imbued with the quality of the sacred. It is to these homely environs that Tóibín returns us, gently hinting – as does Winnicott too – that it is within the folds of the other that the vectors of faith are to be found.

Notes

1 All references in the text to *The Testament of Mary* are taken from Tóibín, C. (2013). *The Testament of Mary*. London: Penguin Books.
2 However, in a footnote to his paper, Ghent (1999) cites Rycroft (1966, p. 22) who 'observed that "there would seem to be no necessary incompatibility between psychoanalysis and those religious formulations which locate God within the self. One could indeed argue that Freud's Id (and even more Groddeck's It), the impersonal force within which is both the core of oneself and yet not oneself, and from which in illness one becomes alienated, is a secular formulation of the insight which makes religious people believe in an immanent God"' (p. 215).

References

Auerbach, F. (1953). *Mimesis. The Representation of Reality in Western Literature*, trans. W.R. Trask. Princeton, NJ: Princeton University Press.
Benveniste, E. (1969). *Le vocabulaire des institutions indo-européennes*, Vol. 1, pp. 87–101. Paris: Les Editions de Minuit.

Bion, W. (1970). *Attention and Interpretation*. London: Tavistock.
Butler, J. (2005). *Giving an Account of Oneself*. New York: Fordham University Press.
Caputo, J. (2006). *The Weakness of God: A Theology of the Event*. Bloomington, IN: Indiana University Press.
Derrida, J. (1995). *The Gift of Death*. Chicago: University of Chicago Press.
Derrida, J. (2000). *Of Hospitality*, trans. R. Bowlby. Palo Alto, CA: Stanford University Press.
Eigen, M. (1999). The area of faith in Winnicott, Lacan and Lacan. In: S. Mitchell and L. Aron (eds), *Relational Psychoanalysis: The Emergence of a Tradition*, pp. 211–242. Hillsdale, NJ: The Analytic Press.
Emerson, R.W. (1850). *Representative Men: Seven Lectures*. Cambridge, MA: Belknap Press, 1996.
Felman, S. (1992). Education and crisis, or the vicissitudes of teaching. In: S. Felman and D. Laub (eds), *Testimony: Crises of Witnessing in Literature, Psychoanalysis and History*. New York: Routledge.
Freud, S. (1923). The ego and the Id. In: J. Strachey (ed. and trans.), *The Standard Edition of the Complete Psychological Works of Sigmund Freud*, Vol. 19, pp. 1–66. London: Hogarth.
Freud, S. (1927). The future of an illusion. In: J. Strachey (ed. and trans.), *The Standard Edition of the Complete Psychological Works of Sigmund Freud*, Vol. 21, pp. 5–55. London: Hogarth.
Ghent, E. (1999). Masochism, submission, surrender: Masochism as a perversion of surrender. In: S. Mitchell and L. Aron (eds), *Relational Psychoanalysis: The Emergence of a Tradition*, pp. 211–242. Hillsdale, NJ: The Analytic Press.
Hodge, B. (2006). The Goddess Tour: Spiritual tourism/post-modern pilgrimage in search of Atlantis. In: L. Hume and K. McPhillips (eds), *The Politics of Contemporary Enchantment*, pp. 22–40. London: Routledge.
Hood, W. (1993). *Fra Angelico at San Marco*. New Haven, CT: Yale University Press.
Kearney, R. (2001). *The God Who May Be. A Hermeneutics of Religion*. Bloomington, IN: Indiana University Press.
Kearney, R. (2010). *Anatheism: Returning to God after God*. New York: Columbia University Press.
Kearney, R. (2015). *Reimagining the Sacred. Richard Kearney debates God*. Eds. R. Kearney and J. Zimmermans. New York: Columbia University Press.
Lacan, J. (2006a). *Le Séminaire. Livre XIII: L'objet de la psychanalyse*, ed. M. Roussan. Unpublished.
Lacan, J. (2006b). *Le Séminaire. Livre XVI: D'un Autre à l'autre*, ed. J-A. Miller. Paris: Seuil.
Levinas, E. (1969). *Totality and Infinity: An Essay on Exteriority*, trans. A. Lingis. Pittsburgh, NJ: Duquesne.
Lloyd, D. and White, D. (1998). *Fra Angelico*, 2nd rev. ed. London: Phaidon Press.
Neri, C. (2005) What is the function of faith and trust in psychoanalysis? *International Journal of Psychoanalysis*, 86, 1: 79–97.
Oppenheimer, M. (2012). Gospel truth: Colm Tóibín reinvents Mary. *The New Republic*. Available at: https://newrepublic.com/article/111314/gospel-colm-Tóibín-mary-jesus-bible (accessed August 16, 2019).

Ostow, M. (1995). Normative religion versus illusion. In: M. Ostow (ed.), *Ultimate Intimacy: The Psychodynamics of Jewish Mysticism*. Madison, CT: International Universities Press.
Pullman, P. (1995). *Northern Lights: His Dark Materials*. London: Scholastic Children's Books.
Rieff, P. (1966). *The Triumph of the Therapeutic. Uses of Faith after Freud*. New York: Harper and Rowe.
Rushdie, S. (1988). *The Satanic Verses*. London: Viking, Penguin.
Rycroft, C. (1966). Causes and meaning. In: C. Rycroft (ed.), *Psychoanalysis Observed*. New York: Coward-McCann.
Safran, J. (1999). Faith, despair, will, and the paradox of acceptance. *Contemporary Psychoanalysis*, 35, 1: 5–23.
Safran, J. (2006). The relational unconscious, the enchanted interior, and the return of the repressed. *Contemporary Psychoanalysis*, 42, 2: 393–412.
Sorenson, R.L. (2004). *Minding Spirituality*. Hillsdale, NJ: Analytic Press.
Spezzano, C. and Gargiulo, G. (2013). *Soul on the Couch. Spirituality, Religion and Morality in Contemporary Psychoanalysis*. New York: Routledge.
Starr, K. (2008). Faith as the fulcrum of psychic change: Metaphors of transformation in Jewish mysticism and psychoanalysis. *Psychoanalytic Dialogues*, 18, 2: 203–229.
Steiner, G. (1989). *Real Presences*. Chicago, IL: University of Chicago Press.
Tóibín, C. (2014a). *The Testament of Mary*. London: Penguin Books.
Tóibín, C. (2014b). How I wrote Mary's story. *Daily Telegraph*, April 16. Available at: https://www.telegraph.co.uk/culture/theatre/10755366/Colm-Toibin-how-I-wrote-Marys-story. html (accessed August 16, 2019).
Treanor, B. (2010). The anatheistic wager: faith after faith. *Religion and the Arts*, 14: 547–560. Warner, M. (2000). *Alone of All Her Sex*. London: Vintage.
Winnicott, D. (1971). The use of an object and relating through identifications. In: *Playing and Reality*, Chapter 6, pp. 101–111. London: Penguin.
Zornberg, A. (1995). *The Beginning of Desire: Reflections on Genesis*. New York: Doubleday.
Zornberg, A. (2002). *The Particulars of Rapture*. New York: Doubleday.

Chapter 3

Psychoanalysis and ways of reading
Henry James's *The Figure in the Carpet*

Introduction

In an interview with Michael Neve in 1983 (Neve, 1992), Claire Winnicott discusses how her husband Donald went straight from university in Cambridge to working as the medical officer in charge of a destroyer in the Navy during the First World War. At one point suggesting that Winnicott, a first year medical student at the time, may have known very little about the job, she confides almost as an aside: 'He had a lot of free time and read the novels of Henry James, as far as I can tell, most of the time. He had a lot of time for reading' (p. 179). It is not altogether surprising that the middle-class, well-educated Winnicott would have had a lot of time for reading; but as psychoanalysts we might want to pause for a moment to imagine why he appears to have been drawn to a writer such as Henry James. Was it simply James's supreme concern with the passage from innocence into adulthood and the painful and costly problems encountered on the path to emotional maturity? Certainly as a psychoanalyst in the making, Winnicott was to develop this same theme in his theoretical writing throughout his life, charting in great and imaginative detail the infant's journey from absolute dependence on maternal care to relative independence based on a hard-won capacity to be alone.

Be that as it may, the imaginative fiction of Henry James has often been considered a particular source of interest for psychoanalysts, with Rivkin (2007) pointing out that James, whilst a 'genius of consciousness is also – and necessarily – the genius of the unconscious' (p. 59). James's writing can be seen to index a preoccupation akin to Freud's with a kind of 'doubling' of the mind; a fascination with how the mind's surface or consciousness acts as barometer of that which remains unseen below. Like the early Freud, James was to become increasingly interested in the eloquence of the unsaid; the way not being able to notice, understand or speak about something can lend it additional psychic weight. In his well-known labyrinthine literary style and complex syntactical constructions conveying the most fine-grained and nuanced of meanings, James imbues his protagonists' tendency to erasure and omission with enormous cumulative emotional force. Indeed, the phenomenology of a confused, partial

DOI: 10.4324/9781003325468-4

and limited understanding is frequently deployed by James as necessary foil to his authorial mastery of allusion, nuance, hint and suggestion. It is surely not a coincidence that these are literary skills Winnicott was himself to adopt in his own, highly idiosyncratic way, nor that he became, like James, capable of provoking considerable exasperation in his readers. But whilst James's endlessly proliferating clauses are often considered overly rarefied and abstruse, it is Winnicott's enigmatic concision that usually frustrates and puzzles his readers. Indeed, Greenberg and Mitchell (1983) argue that Winnicott 'entices, baffles and provokes his readers, valuing them highly but never confronting them directly' (p. 190).

If Winnicott valued his readers, so did James who claimed in 1908: 'In every novel, the work is divided between the writer and the reader; but the writer makes the reader very much as he makes his characters. When he makes him well, that is, makes him interested, then the reader does quite the labour' (p. 18). 'Making the reader' seems to involve the writer's ability to incite a level of interest or curiosity that sets the reader off on the task of what Emerson, before James, once called 'creative reading'. Creative, or close, attentive reading for James is central to an appreciation of his work and deemed interchangeable with what he calls the 'supremely beneficent' art of literary criticism, something he thought demanded a 'rare cluster of qualities': curiosity, sympathy, and 'perception at the pitch of passion' (p. 264). At its best, criticism for James implied the potential presence and attention of the kind of ideal reader he hoped his writing would produce. The Jamesian reader is one who above all has to do 'quite the labour', straining to appreciate the highly-wrought articulation of shades and textures of feelings and thoughts that have rarely been expressed in writing or perhaps even been experienced at all.

But James was distressed to find that appreciation of his work was not always forthcoming. After the humiliating failure of his play *Guy Domville*, he had been left acutely depressed by his encounter with what he called the 'great flat foot of the public' and shortly afterwards set to work on a series of stories he was later to bring together in Volumes XV and XVI of the New York Edition, each of which was concerned with what he called 'the troubled artistic consciousness' (Vol XV, p. xiii). One of the first of these was *The Figure in the Carpet* written in 1896, James's plea is for the kind of sensitive criticism that could 'reinstate analytic appreciation [...] so far as possible, in its virtually forfeited rights and dignities' (1934, p. 228). His story offers an ironic – and wickedly funny – riff on the failure of literary critics and all professional commentators to understand what the writer is trying to do and has since been read and re-read by a series of fascinated critics in a flood of essays, criticism and counter-criticism serving both to mime and respond to James's fable. Zabel argues that the tale is 'a virtual paradigm of James's notion of the creative mystery' (1958, p. 20, quoted in Levy 1962) whilst Levy (1962) tells us that it is 'one of the most bewildering of James's fictions' (p. 457). Rimmon (1977) claims that the story is fundamentally uncertain in meaning, and certainly it is one that is bafflingly enigmatic, attracting multiple ambiguous readings even whilst the text itself seems deliberately to provoke the reader – as dramatised by the luckless narrator in the story – to establish a single, conclusive interpretation. Perhaps for this reason, the story is regarded by Hardy (1988) as a 'trap baited for critics and James's revenge on the reviewers' (p. 87).

James's artistic capacity to provoke the reader to 'do quite the labour' in this particular story is certainly startling and it is precisely in his capacity to provoke and incite the reader to make something of what he or she is reading that I think James's affinity with Winnicott lies. In this chapter, I want to explore what might seem an unlikely kinship between these two writers who, along with the French psychoanalyst Jean Laplanche, seem to be fascinated with how we continually and creatively absorb, rework and revise aspects of our external reality, including the books we read. I hope to elucidate some of what I see as their shared concerns, and to find out not only how James's ideas might be useful to us as readers of psychoanalytic theory but also how psychoanalytic theory might itself thicken and illuminate our understanding of James's ideas about reading. This attempt is not without problems however and I am aware of the need to tread softly on the somewhat fraught relationship that is often said to exist between psychoanalysis and literature. Indeed, as I have suggested in the introduction, the use of psychoanalysis as a conceptual system to 'read' literature has not only come to give certain types of psychoanalytic literary criticism a bad name, but also sustains a fantasy about rival claims to authority that I am anxious to avoid here. Rather, I hope to develop a dialogue between the two domains rather than privileging any one 'reading' over another, and to consider how three very different writers might mutually inform and generate implications for each other.

I want to start by offering a brief outline of *The Figure in the Carpet*, though I must recognise from the outset the impossibility of summarising such a complex, highly-wrought and profoundly ambiguous fable. However, I will use my summary as a basis for thinking about James's tale in tandem with the work of the French psychoanalyst, Jean Laplanche, focusing on his ideas about the enigmatic signifier and its relationship to culture. Along the way, I will also draw on Winnicott's characteristic way of reading and writing psychoanalytic theory, developing my thoughts about reading as a site of encounter with the message of the writer or artist. I will conclude with a brief consideration of the parallels between the figure of the literary critic and the psychoanalyst and their shared concern with promoting and sustaining creativity.

The Figure in the Carpet[1]

James's tale is told through the eyes of a nameless narrator, an ambitious young literary critic of doubtful competence who is attending a weekend house party. He is rather pleased with a review he has recently published of the latest novel written by the well-known author Vereker. He is both delighted and nervous to discover that Vereker has been invited too, and hopes that the writer will have read his piece.

During the party, a guest produces the review for comment and Vereker, not realising that the reviewer is also a guest, dismisses it as 'the usual twaddle' (p. 5). He later apologises to the narrator and agrees to meet him, claiming that neither he nor anyone else has yet seen the 'exquisite scheme' (p. 8) at work in all his books. At their meeting, Vereker tries to explain the nature of his scheme:

> It's the finest fullest intention of the lot, and the application of it has been, I think, a triumph of patience, of ingenuity [...] It stretches, this little trick of mine, from book to book, and everything else, comparatively, plays over the surface of it. The order, the form, the texture of my books will perhaps someday constitute for the initiated a complete representation of it. So it's naturally the thing for the critic to look for.
>
> (p. 8)

James's slow-witted narrator becomes increasingly confused in trying to understand what Vereker means. He wonders whether it is some kind of 'esoteric message' (p. 9), but Vereker responds, crushingly, 'Ah, my dear fellow, it can't be described in cheap journalese' (p. 9). And so the hunt is on for the Figure, something that is both observable and yet unseen: 'the thing's as concrete there as a bird in a cage, a bait on a hook, a piece of cheese in a mouse-trap. It's stuck into every volume [...]. It governs every line, it chooses every word, it dots every i, it places every comma' (p. 9).

Perhaps it is like Vereker himself, of whom, James tells us, 'there was more [...] than met the eye' (p. 11). For the secret seems to involve depth as well as surface; it cannot be seen though it can be experienced. This tantalising paradox pervades the entire novella, where the visible surface or form of the figure merely indexes a radical absence of which the visible is but a sign. The ever-present absence conveyed by James suggests that the putative existence of the figure itself is perhaps less important than the way in which various characters in the novella subsequently choose to search for it. Two protagonists join the narrator in his relentless search for Vereker's secret. We are told that George Corvick, the narrator's editor, 'followed the chase for which I myself had sounded the horn' (p. 14), as well as the writer, Gwendolen Erme, with whom Corvick has a romantic understanding despite her mother's disapproval. Learning from the narrator that Corvick too is trying to access his 'exquisite scheme', Vereker hints that marriage might help him work it out. Indeed, for Corvick and Gwendolen 'literature was a game of skill, and skill meant courage, and courage meant honour, and honour meant passion, meant life' (p. 18). The narrator is not only envious of the way Corvick is able to 'excite himself over a question of art' (p. 14), but of how both he and

Gwendolen make their pursuit of the figure a central part of their intimate lives together. Meanwhile, the celibate narrator struggles on alone, convinced he will discover the 'buried treasure' (p. 17).

In his portrayal of the relationships between these three main characters, we can discern James's interest in several central themes. Firstly, we are offered an ironic commentary not simply on the different ways of understanding a novel or text, but rather on the possibility of different ways of reading; a difference incarnated in his portrayal of the sexually mature, generous and sophisticated Corvick on the on hand, and his baffled, naïve and celibate narrator on the other. From the outset, the narrator's personal limitations and inexperience are pitted against Corvick's 'supersubtlety' (p. 11). Whilst the narrator becomes increasingly frustrated by his inability to 'get at' Vereker, Corvick who is also fascinated by the literary enigma posed by Vereker, has an aesthetic appreciation that the narrator starts to realise he lacks. 'I was freshly struck with my colleague's power to excite himself over a question of art' muses the narrator. 'He'd call it letters, he'd call it life, but it was all one thing' (p. 14). In pursuit of the Figure, however, it is clear that the narrator doesn't actually spend much time reading at all. Instead, he makes a greedy and increasingly futile grab at Vereker's novels, trying to absorb what he imagines is their meaning as quickly as possible: 'Returning to town I feverishly collected them all; I picked out each in its order and held it up to the light. This gave me a maddening month' (p. 10). His ill-fated attempt is soon given up however, and James instead tells us about a quite different way of reading in his portrayal of the relationship between Corvick and Gwendolen. The couple become increasingly involved in reading Vereker and it is clear that not only do they do so more slowly and thoughtfully, but also that the act of reading is for them a joint activity:

> They did as I had done, only more deliberately and sociably – they went over their author from the beginning. There was no hurry. Corvick said the future was before them and the fascination could only grow; they would take him page by page [...] inhale him in slow draughts and let him sink all the way in.
>
> (p. 14)

This slow absorption of Vereker's work, a refusal to hurry, and the generative quality of close, attentive reading that promises a future yield are all aspects of reading that James points to as significant.

Secondly, it is clear that James wants us to understand that the sexual relationship between Corvick and Gwendolen is something that promotes this latter kind of reading. During the story, we learn that the couple's engagement is unexpectedly broken off and Corvick goes to India, leaving the narrator and Gwendolen at home. After several months, Gwendolen receives a sudden cable, dramatically announcing that Corvick has at last discovered the meaning of Vereker's work: *'Eureka. Immense'* (p. 18) is all it says and Gwendolen immediately cables the excited narrator to tell him the news, later explaining that 'the thing itself' (p. 18) will be revealed fully only after she marries Corvick on his return. James seems to link the promised fruits of literary success to sexual consumption, even telling us that Gwendolen believes that Corvick's determination to withhold the secret until after they are married is 'tantamount to saying – isn't it? – that I must marry him straight off!' (p. 20). When Corvick is subsequently killed in an accident on the couple's honeymoon, the narrator's obsession for locating Vereker's secret meaning even leads him briefly to consider marrying Gwendolen himself: 'Was the figure in the carpet traceable or describable only for husbands and wives – for lovers supremely united?' (p. 25). Indeed, James hints that the narrator's solitary existence, pursuing the figure at the expense of living a sexually fulfilled and meaningful life, exempts him from reaching the literary understanding he is so determined to find. Eventually, on a visit to the widowed Gwendolen, he finds the courage to ask her what she knows, only to find to his despair that Gwendolen refuses to tell him, responding with 'the largest, finest, coldest "Never"' (p. 25). He subsequently reads her second novel in the hope of finding some trace of what he is seeking, but disconsolately realises 'the figure was not the figure I was looking for' (p. 26).

Finally, we learn that everyone in the story whom the narrator believes to be initiated into the secret dies, the theme of death deployed by James here to signify the unachievable nature of the quest undertaken by his protagonists. Following Corvick's death, Vereker dies abroad followed by his ailing wife. Gwendolen remarries, this time to another critic, Drayton Deane, and subsequently dies herself in childbirth, leaving the narrator 'shut up in my obsession forever – my gaolers had gone off with the key' (p. 28). Assuming that Deane, as Gwendolen's widower, will be the last remaining person in possession of the knowledge he so desperately pursues, the narrator finally tracks him down to question him about the figure. James allows Deane to deliver the devastating final blow: 'I don't know what you're talking about' (p. 30); and our forlorn narrator is left to assume either that Deane is insufficiently intelligent to have been entrusted with the secret, or that he too will want to join the narrator in his unquenchable desire for the figure. Either way, James leaves his unfortunate narrator sealed up forever within his obsessive quest for meaning.

Ways of reading

Why does James's narrator fail to 'get at' the figure? Indeed, how might we understand the 'figure' in the first place? Miller (1980) points out that the term 'figure' is used by James to refer both to the 'figures' or characters in the story and for the notion of relationship between them, going on to suggest that 'the human story is the metaphor of the figure, which, paradoxically, is the literal object of the story, though it is a literal which could never be described or named literally' (pp. 110–11). The narrator's metaphysical pursuit of 'an idea, a design, a general and organizing intention' (p. 111) for which there are no literal terms confirms that he is, from the outset, engaged in the Jamesian quest for Knowledge; for what Todorov calls, in a discussion of James's fiction, 'an absolute and absent cause' (Todorov and Weinstein, 1973, p. 73). In order to provoke the hunt, the figure must be always absent and invisible even though its presence haunts and underwrites everything that happens in the narrative. But in reading James's fable, we find ourselves taking up the position of his narrator confronted with the paradox of an absence which is continually present and which, as Halter (1984) argues in Lacanian vein, continually defers meaning and thus any successful resolution of the narrator's conundrum. In the end, like the narrator, we are neither able to tell whether there is any figure to find, nor why James wanted to pose the dilemma in the first place. Indeed, one of the many ironies conveyed by James in his novella is that in our baffled attempts to wrest meaning from the heart of the story, we become enmeshed in the very trap James's wretched narrator is unable to resist.

It is worth quoting James's (1934) Preface to *The Figure in the Carpet* in full here:

> I came to Hugh Vereker, in fine, by this travelled road of a generalisation; the habit of having noted for many years how strangely and helplessly, among us all, what we call criticism – its curiosity never emerging from the limp state – is apt to stand off from the intended sense of things [...] Vereker's drama [...] is that at a given moment the limpness begins vaguely to throb and heave, to become conscious of a comparative tension. As an effect of this mild convulsion acuteness, at several points, struggles to enter the field and the question that accordingly comes up, the issue of the affair, can be but whether the very secret of perception hasn't been lost.
> (p. 229)

In this remarkable and sexually suggestive piece of writing, James points to a relationship between the writer who intends to convey something and the reader/critic who receives it as potentially an erotic one; yet one that is nonetheless in danger of never emerging 'from the limp state'. Limpness here seems to refer to a lack of sensitivity or what James calls 'acuteness', as if the reader is oblivious, failing utterly to be curious or excited about what it is the writer is attempting to convey; worse, failing even to notice that there is something to *be* conveyed, as dramatised by James's dismayed, and dismaying, narrator. But what James goes on to draw attention to is that at the moment the reader's curiosity is piqued, just as a 'comparative tension' arises, there is a struggle, a conflict. We see this conflict played out in the encounter between the 'cheap journalese' used by James's narrator to pin down, describe and locate the figure and the kind of refined sensibility that is exemplified by

Corvick's 'supersubtlety'; as if 'the question that accordingly comes up' for James is one of whether we are able at all, as readers, to notice, pay attention, be conscious of what is indirect and elusive. James seems to be drawing attention here to that which resists definition in the text, something which is in danger of disappearing entirely in our attempts to articulate, label and define it.

The very 'secret of perception' appears to lie in the particular kind of sensibility that is needed to detect and establish the writer's meaning. In his essay *Criticism*, James (1893) had already articulated the constellation of qualities he deemed necessary in the reader/critic whom he saw acting as companion to the writer's intentions: 'To lend himself, to project himself, to feel and feel till he understands, and to understand so well that he can say, to have perception at the pitch of passion' (p. 264). This is a significant statement from James who seems to be telling us that it is feeling that leads to understanding, not the reverse. Rather than constituting the opposite pole to cognition and understanding as is frequently thought to be the case, feeling and passion instead underpin them. Sexual passion, of course, is famous for rendering those involved blind to judgement and thought; yet James nonetheless makes a claim here for the primacy of feeling and desire, something he illustrates in the relationship that Corvick and Gwendolen cement over their ardent love of literature. More, the passionate coupling of the lovers that leads them to literary understanding is mirror image of the passionate relationship between reader and text that leads to what James (1934) calls in his Preface to *The Lesson of the Master* 'the beautiful Gate itself of enjoyment' (p. 227). Reading, for James, thus seems to be akin to a love affair in which the reader's consciousness is, like Corvick and Gwendolen, 'supremely united' with the work of literature and the portrayal of life that it offers. And so James's slow-witted narrator fails to perceive Vereker's artistic intention not simply because of a lack of intelligence or literary scholarship so much as his inability to move beyond a certain kind of emotional sterility. He is unable fully, passionately and profoundly to engage with the work of literature and so the relationship is destined to remain forever unconsummated.

The passionate engagement with the text that James advocates seems to enact a process parallel to that of artistic creativity. The erotic stands as metaphor here not only for the kind of reading that James is interested in, but also for the very source of artistic inspiration that first stimulated and now imbues the text. In his Preface to *The Spoils of Poynton*, James (1934) mentions what he calls 'the virus of suggestion' (p. 119), the merest hint or germ of a story stumbled on in casual conversation that in his mind comes to form the basis of a subsequent tale. Miming its erotic impact via further use of sexually allusive vocabulary, James goes on to refer to 'the stray suggestion, the wandering word, the vague echo at the touch of which the novelist's imagination winces as at the prick of some sharp point: its virtue is all in its needle-like quality, the power to penetrate as finely as possible (p. 119). As writer and critic, James wants to be – in fact, insists on being – intensely receptive to something almost imperceptible, a 'vague echo' in the surrounding atmosphere, a signifier to which his 'supersubtle' hearing is highly attuned, acutely sensitive. It is something charged with an excess of meaning that, sharp as a needle, punctures – or 'penetrates', as James says in rather less ambiguous terms – his consciousness and gets the quest for meaning going in his imagination. It is as if the text becomes infected by the 'virus of suggestion', something that James passes on to the reader who may, in his or her turn, become as gripped, enthralled and captivated as the hapless narrator of *The Figure in the Carpet*.

The figure and the enigmatic signifier

In James's fable, the erotic is that 'sharp point' which acts to incite, to invite interest. In its very ambiguity, it acts as irresistible spur to the reader to try to understand and make sense of the story. Indeed, it could be argued that *The Figure in the Carpet* throws down a kind of textual gauntlet, setting the reader off – or up, perhaps – on his or her quest for elucidation. And so I want to suggest that James's story illuminates and embodies something that literature has the potential to do: to invite, solicit and seduce the reader. Our curiosity 'throbs and heaves'; the text, as it were, goads the reader into a response.

This agitating property of a text that James dramatises in his novella is something with which the French psychoanalyst Jean Laplanche was to become concerned nearly a century later. Like Winnicott, Laplanche appears at first to be an improbable literary companion to James. However, we might remember his theory of the enigmatic signifier is rooted in James's time, framed as a re-appropriation of Freud's early seduction theory, a model Freud abandoned in 1897 only a year after *The Figure in the Carpet* was published. Freud's subsequent understanding of the psychic trauma of sexuality in the aetiology of the neuroses is significantly reworked in Laplanche's (1999) myth of human origins, where he sees the provocation of the enigmatic, sexual other as constitutive of subjectivity. Our inner lives, Laplanche suggests, are set in motion as infants by the continual stream of what he calls enigmatic 'messages' conveyed by the caregiver and which constitute the scene of so-called primal seduction. This ordinary and inevitable part of development is characterised by a fundamental asymmetry: not only is the fledgling subject biologically dependent on the adult caregiver, but there is a discrepancy in what Laplanche calls the 'communication situation' because unlike the adult, the infant has, as yet, no sexual unconscious. The messages that the adult conveys to the infant are therefore saturated with unconscious sexual significance and are, suggests Forester (1999), doubly enigmatic: 'not just because the infant has no access to a code to determine their meaning, or because they outstrip its capacities for understanding, but because, compromised by the unconscious wishes of the other, they are opaque to the adult as well' (p. 12). In the infant's attempts to assimilate or manage these unfathomable messages transmitted by the adult there is always an excess of representation that cannot be metabolised, a surplus that exceeds the infant's capacity to bind and translate. It is this excess that Laplanche suggests is repressed and forms the basis of the infant's unconscious. The unconscious is therefore the repressed, untranslated (and untranslatable) enigmatic residue of the other, an 'internal foreign body [...]: the unconscious as an alien inside me, and even one put inside me by an alien' (1999, p, 65).

This residue or trace of the other's unconscious within us is puzzling, says Laplanche, because the adult's unwitting transmission of a signal to the infant has become uncoupled from its referent: 'The passage to the unconscious', he writes (1999), 'is correlative with a loss of referentiality' (p. 90). The repressed residue of the other 'loses its status as presentation (as signifier) in order to become a thing which no longer presents (signifies) anything other than itself' (p. 90) and the interrogative function of the signifier means that whilst it addresses the subject, it doesn't represent or signify anything specific. In other words, the enigmatic message comes to mean something to the child without the adult (or the child) necessarily realising precisely what is being conveyed: 'The signifier may be designified without thereby losing its ability to signify to' (p. 45). The child is thus constitutively ill-equipped to understand what the adult's message might signify, for the code that might determine its translation is lacking. All that remains is a puzzling message that appears to be aimed at, intended for, signifying *to* the child. It is as if the adult inadvertently provides the child with a question to which there is no answer, a question which the child will thereafter ceaselessly attempt yet forever fail to understand, bind and come to terms with. This is precisely the condition of James's unfortunate narrator, who remains baffled and confounded by the question of Corvick and Gwendolen's sexual connection and its implied relationship to knowledge and the meaning of literature. All he is dimly and jealously aware of is an intimacy between them from which he is excluded; their involvement in 'a pastime too precious to be shared with the crowd' (p. 13) is puzzlingly but inextricably linked to their 'infatuation' (p. 14) with Vereker's text.

In his reworking of Freud's metapsychology, Laplanche deploys a cosmic metaphor, aligning the other with the Copernican relocation of the sun to the centre of the solar system whilst Freud's psycho-sexual paradigm is metaphorically affiliated with Ptolemy's geocentric model in which the earth is firmly placed at the centre of the universe. Laplanche sees the infant as ineluctably caught up in the gravitational 'pull' of the other's message, helpless to resist the adult's opaque, sexually-saturated messages rather as the narrator is helplessly in thrall to Vereker's 'primal plan'. But following on from this Copernican openness to the enigmatic other around whom we orbit, there is always a countervailing Ptolemaic tendency to closure, to repression, an attempt to bring the enigma under control: 'the dominant tendency', says Laplanche (1999), 'is always to relativize the discovery and to re-assimilate and reintegrate the alien, so to speak' (p. 65). In psychoanalysis, this may take the form of what Laplanche calls the 'filled-in transference': the patient's familiar self-constructions, the narratives by which he or she has lived that bind the signifier to a well-rehearsed and reassuring self-identity. The work of psychoanalysis, suggests Laplanche (1999), is to reopen the originary situation, to maintain our Copernican openness to the enigma so that these 'old, insufficient, partial and erroneous' (p. 164) translations (the translations of translations which the subject is continually reworking), can give way to fresh ideas and different understandings. The analyst's job, he argues, is to maintain a space for the 'hollowed out transference' through which the 'dimension of alterity' (p. 230) can be maintained and reworked.

James shows a similar concern with the consequences of this tendency to closure, this domestication of the enigmatic psychic nucleus within. In the efforts of his hapless narrator, James caricatures the futile attempt to continually reduce the mystery of Vereker's story to 'vulgar' clichés and second hand phrases borrowed from other reviewers. James is far more interested in the possibility of a radical openness to the world that is beyond our capacity to reduce it to what is already known. It is precisely this acute awareness of alterity that he portrays in Corvick's 'supersubtlety' whose unconscious is sensitive to the 'whiffs and hints', the 'faint wandering notes of a hidden music' (p. 15) in a way that the narrator's is not.

Laplanche sees subjectivity as the continual attempt throughout life to translate and retranslate these baffling messages deposited by our parents or caregivers. But in an interesting shift, he suggests that psychoanalysis is not the only or even the most important site of the subject's efforts to re-describe, symbolise or translate the enigmatic trace of the other within. 'If one accepts', he writes (1999), 'that the fundamental dimension of transference is the relation to the enigma of the other, perhaps the principal site of transference, 'ordinary' transference, before, beyond or after analysis, would be the multiple relation to the cultural, to creation or, more precisely, to the cultural message' (p. 222). Laplanche is arguing here that a central characteristic of the cultural is an address to 'the nameless crowd' (p. 224) who will receive the 'message in the bottle' (p. 48) that is cast out by the artist to 'others scattered in the future' (p. 224). The cultural thus constitutes an intrusive and sexually stimulating enigma that is received by the anonymous future addressee without the artist or writer explicitly addressing anyone in particular. Just as transference constitutes a re-opening of the originary situation of primal seduction, so too, suggests Laplanche (1999), the book, the work of art, the film or the symphony provokes a response in the recipient or addressee who is ineluctably pulled into the orbit of its unconscious message: something that 'repeats the originary situation of the human being' (p. 83).

Of course, as Stack (2005) has pointed out, there can be a range of responses to the cultural enigmatic signifier. After the failure of *Guy Domville*, James knew only too well that not everyone is equally sensitive to the 'vague echo' of the artist's intentions. Both James and Laplanche, albeit in different ways, are curious about what we might call the fate of the cultural message, the 'whiffs and hints' from the work of art that find a passage to the public's ears and eyes. Laplanche (1999) offers a theoretical outline of what he sees as the fate of the unconscious message where it can either be left untranslated, becoming a persecutory communication incarnated by the individual's superego, or it may be successfully repressed, continuing as a troublesome splinter lodged within in the individual's unconscious. In this latter version of repression, the text or work of art comes to be enclosed by a 'Ptolemaic' translation that domesticates its enigmatic qualities. Like James's narrator, the individual merely rehearses and recycles prior ideas and critiques. But in a third vicissitude, Laplanche (2014) refers to 'a repression, but one that preserves the sharp goad of the enigma' (p. 96); a form of repression that nonetheless maintains a 'Copernican' opening to the enigma that allows the individual to remain 'available to the other who comes to surprise me' (p. 98). It is this encounter with the 'sharp goad of the enigma' that James is able to stage for us so evocatively in *The Figure in the Carpet*: a staging that aligns us with the protagonists in order that we too may be pulled into the orbit of that 'vague echo', the 'needle-like' artistic message that James wants us continually to ponder.

Criticism, psychoanalytic theory, and reading

'There is then creative reading as well as writing', claims Emerson (1837, p. 59); and so the act of reading books for James and the (rather different) psychoanalytic act of 'reading' people for Laplanche could be said, in the reading of these two writers that I am developing here, to share a common creative endeavour: one that requires a 'supersubtle' sensitivity, an alertness to the 'virus of suggestion' and a willingness to read in a way that sustains a 'Copernican' receptivity or openness to new possibilities, fresh nuances, and shades and refinements of meaning within the story.

But what might this mean for that class of literature we call psychoanalytic theory? 'In a certain manner', writes Laplanche (1999), 'analytic theory is in this respect a metatheory in relation to the fundamental theorisation that all human beings carry out: not primarily in order to appropriate Nature, but to bind anxiety in relation to the trauma that is the enigma' (p. 132). If psychoanalytic theory is what Freud invented in order to manage or make sense of what is mysterious, what cannot be understood or consciously thought about, what does this mean for how it should be read? It may be appropriate – even enjoyable – to read imaginative literature inventively, but we tend to think rather differently when it comes to the psychoanalytic literature. Indeed, psychoanalytic theory is generally something we tend to read more out of duty than pleasure, partly because psychoanalysis has always been rather protectionist about its theoretical lineage. Its history has been riven with well-known disputes over the literature and who, following Freud, had the right to convey, teach and disseminate its central tenets and doctrines. The extraordinarily divisive wrangling in the wartime Controversial Discussions within the British Psycho-Analytic Society that took place over the introduction of Melanie Klein's ideas within the Freudian community was perhaps emblematic of its tendency to adopt what Roustang aptly calls a theological reading of Freud. (Roustang's (1986) own grim literary masterpiece, *Dire Mastery*, suggests this historical obeisance to Freud, and later, in France, to Lacan, was linked to power disputes within psychoanalytic institutions that continue to find a powerful counterpart in arguments over the standing and status of psychoanalysis today.)

Against this troubled historical backdrop, then, we can begin to understand why the critical reception that greeted the presentation of Winnicott's paper to the British Psychoanalytic Society in November of 1952 was so decidedly chilly. Winnicott's paper was called – not co-incidentally perhaps – 'Anxiety Associated with Insecurity' and was intended as a response to a paper given earlier that year by Charles Rycroft on vertigo. In his paper, Winnicott set out to elaborate on the importance of the mother's function in giving her baby a feeling of security, and in his characteristically playful style made the following comment to his colleagues: 'I found myself saying to this society (about ten years ago) and I said it rather excitedly and with heat: 'There is no such thing as a baby' (p. 99). Of course, in drawing attention to the mother's good-enough care of her infant, Winnicott knew that he was flying in the face of the Kleinian orthodoxy that privileges and prioritises internal unconscious phantasy. 'Anxiety', he daringly suggested, 'can be prevented with good enough care [...] the unit is not the individual, the unit is an environment-individual set-up. The centre of gravity of the being does not start off in the individual. It is in the total-set-up' (p. 99). Winnicott's paper was roundly criticised during the meeting. Afterwards, in a letter to Klein, he wrote:

> I personally think that it is very important that your work should be restated by people discovering in their own way and presenting what they discover in their own language. It is only in this way that the language will be kept alive. If you make the stipulation that in future only your language shall be used for the statement of other people's discoveries then language becomes a dead language as it has already become in the Society [...] The worst example perhaps, was C's paper in which he simply bandied about a lot of that which has now come to be known as Kleinian stuff without giving any impression of the processes personal to the patient. One felt that if he were growing a daffodil he would think that he was making the daffodil out of a bulb instead of enabling the bulb to develop into a daffodil by good enough nurture.
> (Winnicott 1952b)

All orthodoxies, including psychoanalytic ones, insist on imposing a single language. For Winnicott, the compulsory use of Kleinian or any other kind of theoretical language risked stifling creativity and growth. If theoretical language can't be pulled about, played with, attacked or 'destroyed', as he might have said, then it dies off; it ceases to be useful, viable, vital. In Laplanchean terms, theoretical orthodoxy incarnates the Ptolemaic re-centring of the enigma that is thereby domesticated into something known, familiar, rehearsed. Perhaps it is not surprising for a clinician so committed to playfulness, spontaneity and authenticity that Winnicott was particularly opposed to what he saw as the analytic rigidity and docile obedience of many of his colleagues within the British Institute of Psychoanalysis and was determined to defend his right to rework 'Kleinian stuff' in his own words and in his own way. Winnicott was notoriously reluctant to reference other thinkers and writers and it was quite usual for him not to acknowledge what he borrowed from his rivals and precursors within the psychoanalytic cannon. His version of Freudian and Kleinian metapsychology is highly idiosyncratic, and his allusions and ideas are couched in terms that render them all but unrecognisable. He was, of course, well aware of his capacity to absorb, assimilate and transform theoretical ideas from other people. In 1945, he writes:

> I shall not first give an historical survey and show the development of my ideas from the theories of others, because my mind doesn't work that way. What happens is that I gather this and that, here and there, settle down to clinical experience, form my own theories and then, last of all, interest myself in looking to see where I stole what. Perhaps this is as good a method as any.
> (Winnicott 1945a, p. 145)

Winnicott, like James, seems to be alert to the 'virus of suggestion' which, for him, emerges vividly within psychoanalytic theory. Like James, he gathers 'this and that', refashioning it according to his own clinical experience, not worrying about where it comes from. If, as James (1934) suggests, '[t]o criticize is to appreciate, to appropriate, to take intellectual possession, to establish in fine a relation with the criticized thing and to make it one's own' then we could say that Winnicott is Klein's best critic, seizing possession of her ideas in order to rework and reweave them into the fabric of his own developing theories. Like Harold Bloom's (1973) 'strong poet', he insists on the right to deliberately 'misread' his analytic rivals and precursors in a way that marks out a distinctive, new and creative place for himself. 'I have an irritating way of saying things in my own language', he writes in a letter to Anna Freud in 1945, 'instead of learning how to use the terms of psychoanalytic metapsychology' (Winnicott 1945b, p. 58). By modifying, adapting and revising the prevailing theories of the day, by framing them in his allusive, paradoxical and playful language, Winnicott manages to keep a sense of discovery, of creativity, alive and in circulation.

Of course, you don't have to be a psychoanalyst to recognise, as I suspect Winnicott did, that there is often something peculiarly dense, inscrutable and puzzling about many psychoanalytic texts. Like the narrator in *The Figure in the Carpet*, we are often left to wonder whether there is 'evidently [...] something to be understood' in these frequently baffling tracts. Perhaps it is precisely this indecipherable quality that sponsors the kind of Ptolemaic recentring that Laplanche sees as an effort to domesticate the enigma of alterity. So when Winnicott remarks that 'C. bandied about a lot of that which has now come to be known as Kleinian stuff', he is referring to the way his colleague appears have sold his own original views, his psychoanalytic birthright as it were, for a mess of Klein: rehashing his psychoanalytic ideas to fit within an already known and familiar theoretical language. Reading theory in this way all too easily acts to domesticate alterity, providing a Ptolemaic vehicle for re-affirming and buttressing professional credentials, affiliations and identities. Winnicott, rather like James, wants us to engage with something far less complacent and much more uncertain; his insistence on ambiguity, allusion and playfulness – 'there's no such thing as a baby' for example is a Winnicottian phrase artfully posed more as riddle than fact – ensures the reader is not freighted with some kind of presumed 'knowledge' or psychoanalytic orthodoxy but is rather left free to contemplate fresh possibilities for thinking and experiencing. In pointing towards a way of reading that sustains a 'Copernican' opening – 'paradox' being Winnicott's favourite word for this – we are endlessly provoked into further translations, further possibilities, further meaning making.

I am now at the point of suggesting that in Winnicott's reading and writing of psychoanalysis we can begin to discern the enigmatic trace of James, the writer he read so much of as a young man. Both writers reveal to us the importance of the reader's hospitality to that which is strange or other within the text, and both convey the significance of this welcome in a form and language that allows us as readers to live an experience in the act of reading; a miming that seems to enact and make luminous the call to 'Copernican' receptivity under discussion. In *The Figure in the Carpet*, we ourselves participate in the narrator's increasingly baffled search for meaning, feeling his bewilderment and frustration as our own even as we simultaneously recognise the hunt to be futile. This paradoxical awareness does not prevent us from being caught in the very bind James's narrator incarnates; it is in fact constitutive of it, for as we read, the words of the text seem to lodge within us and we are swept up in the chase for which James has himself sounded the horn. Perhaps this is the psychic consequence of the passionate sort of reading that James advocates, a reading in which the words, thoughts and ideas of the writer act as a kind of erotic charge within us, penetrating and mating with the reader's own thoughts, feelings and imagination: 'lovers', like Corvick and Gwendolen, 'supremely united'. Put another way, whilst the text may convey the writer's thoughts, we do not experience them as such; rather, we experience them *as our own*. Although it is I who may be reading the text, it is almost as if I cede to something or someone else; I surrender, as it were, to another self, another 'I'; one to whom I make myself, in the very act of reading, highly permeable. As readers, then, we are not simply gripped or enthralled by a book; we are to a large extent taken over and dispossessed of ourselves. It is as if the book appropriates, even commandeers our consciousness such that the writer's thoughts, actions and feelings temporarily usurp our own. When we read in this way, we are truly, in Laplanche's terms, 'decentred': we surrender once again to an originary situation in which the enigmatic, psychic forcefield of the other is primary.

This extraordinary achievement of literature – the implantation of an unseen, even long-dead other into the psyche, the self – is obviously and quintessentially a preoccupation for the kind of psychoanalysis that takes the other as primary locus of subjectivity. It is not surprising then that Winnicott (1958) went on to develop his ideas about anxiety into a subsequent paper 'The Capacity to be Alone'. Alone for Winnicott, means alone in the presence of a mother who doesn't make any demands on the child, who doesn't impinge or interrupt the child's growing autonomy. This permits a 'potential space' in which the child is able to begin to sort out what is 'me' and what is 'not me' and to become interested in, absorbed by and involved with a world beyond his or her omnipotence. Whilst for Winnicott the archetypal absorption of the child is in play, I would like to suggest that it is only a short time later that the absorption of the child at play evolves into the rapt absorption of the child *reading*. In order to read, and to read passionately as James urges us to do, perhaps we first need the experience of *being alone with someone*; being alone in the presence of mother becomes the prototype, the template, for reading alone in the presence of the text or author. It is in this potential space of reading that we encounter – and re-encounter again and again – the experience of being alone, and yet not alone; where we are once again in the company of an absence: an absence which, like the figure, is continually present. And it is the quality of our relationship to that presence-in-absence, our receptivity to what is enigmatically both 'there' but 'not there', what is self and what is other, that Winnicott deems crucial not only to cultural experience, but to creative living more generally.

Conclusion

The figure of the literary critic, or critic as ideal reader, is one that haunts James's early work. Like Winnicott's child playing alone in the presence of mother, James too sees an imagined companion as essential to the creative process: '[O]ne sees the critic as the real helper of the artist', he writes, 'a torch-bearing outrider, the interpreter, the brother. The more the tune is noted and the direction observed the more we shall enjoy the convenience of a critical literature' (1893, p. 264). The artist, the creator, suggests James, needs his work, his message or '*donnee*' to be seen, to be noticed; in fact, we might say that it is in the imagined eyes and sensitivity of the ideal reader that the entire inspiration for the artistic work resides. The fantasy of the critic/audience becomes itself a kind of enigmatic provocation to the writer, just as the book, the play, the work of art becomes a provocation to the public and particularly to the critic. One of the implications of *The Figure in the Carpet* seems to be the unusual responsibilities borne by the critic who is professionally charged not only with receiving the message of the artist, but also with conveying his or her understanding or interpretation of it to the public. How to do this in a way that maintains the 'sharp goad' of the artistic message, rather than diluting it by resorting to what Laplanche describes as 'old, insufficient, partial and erroneous' interpretations is the task that James sees as central to the critic's vocation.

If this potential space of reading can, to borrow Winnicott's (1971) words, 'be looked upon as sacred to the individual in that it is here that the individual experiences creative living' (p. 121), then it is scarcely surprising that for James the critic holds a sacred vocation as the writer's addressee who is charged with responsibility for provoking the creativity constitutive of artistic life. 'His life, at this rate', admits James (1893), 'is heroic, for it is immensely vicarious. He has to understand for others, to answer for them; he is always under arms [...] he deals with life at second-hand as well as at first; that is, he deals with the experience of others, which he resolves into his own' (p. 265). This could just as well be a description of the psychoanalyst who might equally be thought of as 'under arms', and who 'deals with the experience of others, which he resolves into his own'. For Laplanche, the provocation of the artistic message to which the critic responds is paralleled by the provocation of the psychoanalyst to whom the patient responds. Both culture and psychoanalysis constitute sites of alterity in which a 'Copernican' opening to rather than a 'Ptolemaic' reversal of the enigmatic qualities of the unconscious message may be invited, promoted and sustained. Indeed, the end of a psychoanalysis, Laplanche (2014) argues, is indexed by the possibility of 'the transference of the relation to the enigma as such' (p. 102) where a shift to other cultural sites of inspiration and alterity may start to occur. Rather than this implying the usual kind of object loss and mourning, Laplanche (2014) sees it as the occasion of a continued, future possibility of 'being surprised, seized, traversed by the endless questioning of whoever comes to encounter us' (p. 102).

The capacity to be surprised by new experiences, to chance upon fresh sources of inspiration, to continually refine, revise and find new meanings within what we read and what we experience is central to all the ideas about reading and creativity I have attempted to bring together in this chapter. Indeed, the potentially limitless sources of inspiration and creativity are what make us artists of our own lives: magpies, as it were, thieving otherness from wherever we can find it in order to creatively establish and re-establish a self within. If the possibility of limitless meaning-making is what lends psychoanalysis its always unfinished dimension, it is also what permeates James's (1934) decidedly enigmatic ending to his Preface to *The Figure in the Carpet*:

... the question that accordingly comes up, the issue of the affair, can be but whether the very secret of perception hasn't been lost. That is the situation, and *The Figure in the Carpet* exhibits a small group of well-meaning persons engaged in a test. The reader is, on the evidence, left to conclude.

(p. 229)

Note

1 All references in the text to *The Figure in the Carpet* are taken from James, H. (1896). *The Figure in the Carpet*. CreateSpace Independent Publishing Platform (2016).

References

Bloom, H. (1973). *The Anxiety of Influence: A Theory of Poetry*. New York: OUP.
Emerson, R.W. (1837). The American scholar. In: *Essays and Lectures of Ralph Waldo Emerson*, p. 59. Library of America.
Forester, J. (1999). Introduction. In Laplanche, J., *Essays on Otherness*, pp. 1–51. London: Routledge.
Greenberg, J. and Mitchell, S. (1983). *Object Relations in Psychoanalytic Theory*, p. 89. Cambridge, MA: Harvard University Press,
Halter, P. (1984). Is Henry James's 'The Figure in the Carpet' unreadable? In: Anthony Mortimer (ed.), *Contemporary Approaches to Narrative*. Tubingen: G. Narr.
Hardy, B. (1988). Henry James: imagining imagination. Sarah Tryphena Phillips Lecture. In: *Proceedings of the British Academy*, LXXIV: 71–87. Oxford University Press, 1990.
James, H. (1893). *Essays in London and Elsewhere*, pp. 259–266. New York: Harper Brothers.
James, H. (1896). *The Figure in the Carpet*. CreateSpace Independent Publishing Platform (2016).
James, H. (1908). The novels of George Eliot. In: Le Roy Phillips (ed.), *Views and Reviews*, p. 18. Boston: The Ball Publishing Company.
James, H. (1934). *The Art of the Novel: Critical Prefaces by Henry James*. Chicago and London: University of Chicago Press, 2011. James, H. (1958). *In the Cage and Other Tales*, ed. and introduction by Morton Dawen Zabel. New York: Norton.
Laplanche, J. (1999). *Essays on Otherness*. London: Routledge. Laplanche, J. (2014). Sublimation and/or inspiration. In: John Fletcher and Nicholas Ray (eds), *Seductions and Enigmas. Laplanche, Theory, Culture*, pp. 77–104. London: Lawrence & Wishart.
Levy, L. (1962). A reading of The Figure in the Carpet. *American Literature*, 33, 4: 457–465.
Miller, J.H. (1980). 'The Figure in the Carpet'. *Poetics Today*, 1, 3: 107–118.
Neve, M. (1992). Clare Winnicott talks to Michael Neve. *Free Associations*, 3, 2: 167–184.
Rimmon, S. (1977). *The Concept of Ambiguity – The Example of James*, pp. 22–23. The University of Chicago Press: Chicago and London.
Rivkin, J. (2007). The genius of the unconscious: psychoanalytic criticism. In: Peter Rawlings (ed.), *Palgrave Advances in Henry James Studies*, pp. 59–79. New York: Palgrave MacMillan.

Roustang, F. (1986). *Dire Mastery: Discipleship from Freud to Lacan* (trans. N. Lukacher). American Psychiatric Press.
Stack, A. (2005). Culture, Cognition and Jean Laplanche's Enigmatic Signifier. *Theory, Culture & Society*, 22, 3: 63–80.
Todorov, T. and Weinstein, A. (1973). The structural analysis of literature: the tales of Henry James. In: David Robey (ed.), *Structuralism: An Introduction*, pp. 73–103. Oxford: Clarendon Press.
Winnicott, D. (1945a). Primitive emotional development. In: *Through Paediatrics to Psychoanalysis. Collected Papers*, pp. 145–156. London, Karnac, 1975.
Winnnicott, D. (1945b). Letter to Anna Freud. In: F. Robert Rodman (ed.), *The Spontaneous Gesture. Collected Letters of Donald Winnicott*, p. 58. London, Karnac, 1999.
Winnicott, D. (1952a). Anxiety associated with insecurity. In: *Through Paediatrics to Psychoanalysis. Collected Papers* pp. 97–100. London, Karnac, 1975.
Winnicott, D. (1952b). Letter to Melanie Klein. In: F. Robert Rodman (ed.), *The Spontaneous Gesture. Collected Letters of Donald Winnicott*, p. 35. London, Karnac, 1999.
Winnicott, D. (1958). The capacity to be alone. *International Journal of Psycho-Analysis*, 39: 416–420.
Winnicott, D. (1971). The location of cultural experience. In: *Playing and Reality*. London, Karnac, 1982.

Chapter 4

Epistemologies of the particular
Tessa Hadley's *An Abduction*

Introduction

At the start of Tessa Hadley's short story *An Abduction*,[1] we meet 15-year-old Jane Allsop. She has just returned from her expensive boarding school to spend the long summer holiday at home with her well-to-do parents in 1960s Surrey. In her art classes, she has come across a new word for the colour of the sky: 'cerulean' (p. 1). Jane, we learn, who 'wasn't clever or literary', is 'nervous of new words, which seemed to stick to her' (p. 1); and indeed, the sunny, cerulean sky prises its way 'like a chisel', says Hadley, 'through the crack between Jane's flowered bedroom curtains and between the eyelids she squeezed tightly shut in an effort to stay inside her dreams' (p. 1). From the outset, then, we are being told something about Jane's relationship to knowledge. It makes her uneasy, and no wonder; for the new word she has acquired merely heralds a new and different kind of knowledge that lies in wait for her in 'the fated trek towards adulthood' (p. 4). It will prise its way within, insisting that she see and recognise something however much she wants to close her eyes to it.

We could be forgiven for thinking that we are at the beginning of a good, old-fashioned coming-of-age story. It is a genre with a long tradition that might be said to stretch as far back as the Old Testament and the story of the fall of Adam and Eve. Its many other literary predecessors include Flaubert's (1869) *Sentimental Education*, James's (1897) *What Maisie Knew*, and L. P. Hartley's (1953) *The Go-Between*. Hadley's tale, like Hartley's, is set in the context of a long, broiling hot summer holiday, when a bored, teenaged protagonist removed from the family home to a new, excitingly adult environment is changed forever by an act of sexual betrayal. But Hadley's project extends well beyond portraying the emotional journey from innocence to experience. Rather, I think she wants us to engage with the epistemological implications of that journey: with the nature of what we can know, the means by which we come to know about it and the consequences that will accrue from such knowledge. Hadley makes it clear from the outset that she is not concerned with the kind of knowledge that relates to facts or

DOI: 10.4324/9781003325468-5

theories. This is the kind of academic knowledge that leaves Jane's brother Robin 'blind on his bed with a headache' (p. 3) in an effort to get into Oxford. Perhaps like Jane, he has closed his eyes to the existence of a rather different kind of knowledge: the kind that is hidden, unannounced, unnoticed; the sort of knowledge that is difficult or impossible to speak of, yet which may come to have momentous, even tragic effects on the course of a life.

The story revolves round three central scenes, each located in different places: Jane's home in Surrey; a nearby house to which she is taken for 24 hours; and a counsellor's office, some thirty years later. In the first central scene, Jane is standing in the driveway of her parents' lush garden, listlessly playing Jokari in the blazing summer heat. Ticked off by her father, who secretly worries that she has inherited her mother's troubling 'flat, bland surface' (p. 6), she is subsequently spotted by three boys. They are second-year university students driving by looking for girls to pick up on their way to a weekend house party. As Jane stands there, '[s]omething was revealed in her', writes Hadley, 'that was normally hidden: an auburn light in her face, her freckles startling as the camouflage of an animal [...] She seemed not fake or stuck-up – and, just then in the dappled light, not a child either' (p. 8). Jane's incipient sexuality, camouflaged under her childish freckles, is plainly visible to Daniel, Paddy and Nigel. They are not fooled by Jane's old washed-out dress with its Peter Pan collar, a sartorial clue pointing to Jane's unspoken anxieties about growing up. With only a moment's hesitation, Jane willingly assents to Daniel's invitation to get in the car; and she subsequently takes a further step on the road towards adult desire by allowing herself to be initiated into shoplifting to get wine for an impromptu party that evening. She is already fascinated by Daniel who is 'crushingly beautiful' (p. 9). 'Below the surface of the moment', writes Hadley, 'she began to wait in secret – patiently, for her self-discoveries were very new – for Daniel's hand to jostle her thigh when he changed gears' (p. 11). And so, below the surface of the moment – and below the flat, bland surface of Jane, too – we begin to see the first stirrings of a new kind of knowledge that Jane will, over the next 24 hours, come to reckon with.

As she settles down by the swimming pool in the garden of Nigel's house, Jane becomes intensely and increasingly aware of something that appears to revolve round her feelings for Daniel. When he swears, Jane blushes violently: 'his word was so forbidden that she hardly knew how she knew it [...] It was an entrance, glowering with darkness, into the cave of things unknown to her' (p. 15). Just at this moment, where Jane is hesitating at the entrance of her own desire, the sleek, sexy, sophisticated Fiona, Nigel's 18-year-old sister arrives, creating a sensational and unwelcome distraction. In contrast to Jane's obvious naïveté, here is someone who patently knows all too much. With her new-found knowledge only just beginning to filter through the drawn curtains of her mind, Jane becomes aware that Fiona, by positioning herself at the far end of the terrace to sip her stolen alcoholic drink, is showing off her legs to Daniel through the slit in her sarong.

Ignoring Fiona's play for sexual attention, Daniel has his eye on Jane and seduces her once everyone has gone to the pub. Afterwards, Jane phones home to lie to her mother about where she is, telling her that she will spend the night with a school friend. 'Meanwhile', writes Hadley, 'her own new knowledge filled her up, not in the form of thoughts but as sensations, overwhelming' (p. 23). It is this overwhelming kind of knowledge that will be fully explicated in the second central scene that takes place after Jane and Daniel have fallen asleep together that night. The following morning, Jane wakes up only to find that Daniel has gone. She goes upstairs in search of him and pushes open the door to Nigel's parents' bedroom. Confronting her is a room 'like nothing she'd ever seen before' (p. 24); it is a mise-en-scène replete, saturated, brimming over with knowledge that Jane cannot refuse, and to which she is finally unable to close her eyes. It is a room symbolically filled with light. Unlike her flowered bedroom curtains at home, these curtains are made of translucent linen, allowing the glare of the sun to pour in through the windows onto the huge, white bed, where Daniel and Fiona are lying naked and asleep. 'Jane, who had done the Greeks in history, thought they looked like young warriors in a classical scene, fallen in the place where they had been wrestling. She withdrew from the room without waking them, as quietly as she had come in' (p. 25). Going out into the garden, she stands with 'dry, hot eyes' by the swimming pool, watched by Nigel. After a while, he says quietly: 'So now you know' (p. 25).

Kinds of knowing

But what exactly does Jane know, and what is the nature of the knowledge that she has acquired? We might think of Hadley's dense, highly compressed, dramatic image of the light-filled bedroom as the prototypical scene of knowledge. It portrays the familiar, classical psychoanalytic primal scene, the 'other room' of oedipal knowledge; it is pre-eminently a scene of recognition, of discovery, of what Aristotle, in his *Poetics*, terms anagnorisis. This is one of three constituent elements of 'complex plots', the other elements being peripeteia, or reversal of fortune, and pathos, or suffering. 'Recognition' writes Aristotle 'as the very name shows, is a change from ignorance to knowledge, bringing the characters into either a close bond, or enmity with one another, and concerning matters which bear on their prosperity or affliction' (in Halliwell, 1987, p. 43). For Aristotle, then, the recognition scene is a dramatic device that marks the decisive shift from innocence to experience, playing a crucial role in evoking fear and pity in the audience. It is the moment where something that was previously hidden is now revealed: a moment, writes Cave (1988), 'at which characters understand their predicament fully for the first time [...] it makes the world, and the text, intelligible' (p. 2).

Implied within the etymology and definition of anagnorisis is, significantly, the very idea of knowledge itself. The Greek root word *ana-* means back, again or anew; and so anagnorisis seems to carry within it the sense of knowing something afresh, of knowledge that is not simply gained, but regained. To re-cognise is to know again, to recall or freshly perceive that which was formerly admitted or felt within. Whilst Aristotle leaves open the question of who or what is recognised, Cave's (1988) literary history of the term tells us that in classical versions of anagnorisis, there is a focus on details such as 'the birthmark, the scar, the casket, the handbag' (p. 2): accidental or contingent features of a story on which the recognition of a person's identity depends. In more recent literary use, Cave suggests its meaning extends beyond identification of kinship towards more psychological forms of recognition that emerge in revelatory moments of self-knowledge or self-awareness. In either case, there is a concern with the particulars of a situation: with the exact material, physical or psychological elements that determine exactly how and when the protagonist comes to confer meaning on the situation and through which the truth of him or herself comes to be known.

It is through the particulars of Jane's experience and circumstances – her well-to-do Surrey background, her washed-out dress with its Peter Pan collar, and her growing, baffled and inarticulate awareness of her own sexual nature as well as the existence of a prior sexual relationship between Fiona and Daniel – that we, as readers, come to realise the nature of what she will come to know. For the kind of knowledge that recognition brings, as Aristotle says, 'is what always had to be known because it was from the beginning inscribed in the heart of the tragic action' (in Boitani, 2021, p. 417). Recognition is never really of an identity or an event. It is of *suffering*; and tragedy is set up in such a way that the protagonist is already implicated in his or her suffering before the reasons for this can be fully known. Jane, from the outset, has been repressing knowledge of her blossoming sexuality but this is ultimately something that she will not be able to refuse. Hadley brings her quite literally face-to-face with its implications. Jane is forced to recognise something within herself that was always present, but to which she has previously closed her eyes. Significantly, the knowledge acquired here is not to be obtained through intellectual understanding. Jane's biology lessons at school have not helped her to understand the mystery of sex any more than has doing the Greeks in history. Intellectual scrutiny merely gets in the way of recognising how the scene in the light-filled bedroom confers instantaneous and retrospective meaning on her newly-acquired sexual relationship with Daniel. *Now she knows*. At the same time, she recognises that her desire and pleasure are embedded within a complex adult world, a world of others in which it seems she will not fare well. The fallen warriors in the bed make it clear to Jane that her sexuality positions her within an adult contest for life which is new and full of potential for suffering. Indeed, Jane's is the kind of knowing that is constituted not only by or through sexual experience, but is braided into the suffering it now entails. Hadley implies such knowledge can never be the object of scientific or historical learning, for it cannot be known apart from the pain through which it is delivered. We might say that the shift from innocence to experience here brings about emotional suffering in Jane that constitutes knowing herself in a way that rational, intellectual, systematised forms of knowing do not.

But why should suffering be central to self-awareness? In her essay 'Love's Knowledge', the moral philosopher Martha Nussbaum (1990) makes a distinction between two different means by which we try to achieve self-knowledge. The first is based on a perspective going back to Plato's quarrel between philosophy and poetry and his determination to expel the poets from the Republic. Self-knowledge acquired within the Platonic tradition, Nussbaum suggests, is concerned with trying to understand the self through via a 'detached, unemotional, exact intellectual scrutiny of one's condition, conducted in the way a scientist would conduct a piece of research' (p. 262). Plato proposes separating out reason from emotion, arguing that feelings are an unnecessary distraction from intellectual inquiry. Indeed, he sees feelings as antithetical to any quest for knowledge, misleading reason by derailing and distorting the process by which we seek to know the object of our inquiry. Nussbaum contrasts the idea of knowledge based on the isolation of the intellect with a second kind that is conveyed by the emotions, drawing on the Stoic philosophers' notion of 'cataleptic knowledge'. *Cataleptike* is a Greek term that means 'apprehend' or 'grasp'; and catalepsis refers to certain class of perceptual impressions that by virtue of their vividness intensity and quality, allow us to grasp or know something with a sense of conviction or certainty. A cataleptic impression, says Nussbaum, 'is said to have the power, just through its own felt quality to drag us to assent, to convince us that things could not be otherwise. It is defined', she continues, 'as a mark or impress in the soul' (p. 265) and makes its appearance in a 'blind, unbidden surge of painful affect' (p. 269).

Nussbaum goes on to argue that the kind of knowledge that is based on intellectual self-scrutiny in fact distorts self-knowledge by virtue of the comforting distance it establishes in the effort to be subtle or clever. We protect ourselves from self-knowledge, she argues, by engaging in intellectual games that deter us from deeper or more profound efforts at self-understanding. This becomes evident in the evening after Jane's seduction when Daniel, who is now stoned on methedrine, is sitting by the pool trying to explain to everyone the idea of a soul as understood in Hindu Vedanta. 'What he wanted to describe', writes Hadley, 'was how the soul's origins were in wholeness and light, but on its entry into the world it took on the filth of violence and corruption [...] He believed as he spoke that he was brilliantly eloquent, but in truth he was rambling incoherently' (pp. 22–3). Daniel's clever philosophical attempt to discuss the 'fall' implied by sexual knowledge is, in fact, a rather ostentatious parade of 'brilliant eloquence' that constitutes a refusal of self-knowledge. He imagines he can reach a place of 'wholeness and light', yet in doing so fails to acknowledge the corruption of his own emotions and behaviour. Hadley seems to imply here that the kind of knowledge accruing from an intellect that is so disconnected from emotion will inevitably turn out to be meaningless, even ridiculous: it is merely incoherent rambling.

If the self-deceptions of intellectualisation constitute an obstacle to self-knowledge, it is only the strength of the cataleptic impression that is sufficient to break through our defences, our distancing strategies and our self-deceiving. And this is because the very essence of the cataleptic impression is its pain: sudden, unanticipated, unannounced pain that acts to cut through the comforting distance conferred by the intellect 'as if', says Nussbaum (1990), 'by a surgeon's knife' (p. 269). As we can see when Jane enters that fateful bedroom, anagnorisis, recognition, is that dramatic element that most decisively delivers the cataleptic blow. Suddenly and brutally, she is brought face-to-face with the reality of her position in the world. The object of her love and desire, Daniel, has utterly betrayed her; he is now so evidently beyond her reach and comprehension that Jane has no option other than to silently withdraw and return back home. Significantly, this is not the kind of knowledge that could be obtained in any other way. '[T]he cataleptic impression is not simply a route to knowing', writes Nussbaum; 'it *is* knowing. It doesn't point beyond itself to knowledge; it goes to constitute knowledge' (p. 267). It is Jane's mute suffering, an anguish that speaks only in her 'dry, hot eyes', that itself exposes and constitutes knowledge of her own thwarted desire as well as realisation of her position in the sexual pecking order. The knowing embodied in that moment comes, and can only come, from the felt reality of the situation itself: it is, as it were, its own criterion of validity.

After Nigel drops her back at the foot of her garden at home, Jane looks around her 'as if she'd never seen the place before' (p. 26). Everything is as it was when she left, yet nothing is the same. Her footprints remain intact in the dust of the driveway – even the Jokari bat is where she dropped it – yet Hadley ensures the reader is made aware that Jane's safe return home only serves to mask the disappearance of the girl she was the day before. This disappearance remains unnoticed in the family; and it is clear that Jane herself is anxious to conceal the implications of the weekend's events as much from herself as from her mother. Reverting to her beloved childhood Chalet School story books, she is not even relieved at the early arrival of her menstrual period 'because it hadn't occurred to her until then [...] that she could be pregnant' (p. 26). This inability to link her hard-won emotional knowledge with other kinds of knowledge – her newly acquired sexual experience with what she has learned from her biology lessons for example – does not augur well for Jane's future life and relationships. In a coda of barely three pages, we learn that Jane's silence about what has happened to her will follow her into adulthood; she is never to confide in anyone, not even her husband. Yet we hear too that she will become fearful for her own daughters 'without connecting her fears to anything that had happened to her'. '[I]n a way', writes Hadley, 'she never assimilated the experience, though she didn't forget it either [...] Her early initiation stayed in a sealed compartment in her thoughts and seemed to have no effects, no consequences' (p. 27).

In the highly condensed few lines of a third central scene, however, Jane, by now in her fifties and divorced, visits a counsellor to complain of feeling cut off 'from the real life she was meant to be living' (p. 27). The counsellor, privately irritated by Jane's 'girlish' manner and 'heavy, patient sorrows' (p. 27), asks her what this 'real life' is like. Jane haltingly begins to describe a summer day by the swimming pool and a sun-filled room with a bed on which a naked girl and boy are sleeping. 'I am curled up on the rug beside them', she says, 'The boy turns over, flings out his arm and his hand dangles to the floor [...] I move so that his hand is touching me' (p. 28). In this image, a reworking of the pivotal scene of recognition experienced by the 15-year-old Jane, we witness the moment where the adult Jane's 'flat, bland surface', the 'sealed compartment in her thoughts' (p. 27) at last breaks open. It reveals a fantasy that speaks of unconscious desire that is only just beginning to be voiced and explored. 'That's more like it', thinks the counsellor, 'that's something' (p. 28). In the counsellor's office, Jane is once again on the verge of entering 'the cave of things unknown to her'. It is another scene of recognition, this time a potentially therapeutic one through which the events of her adolescence – which we, as readers, can see have shaped the contours of her life - may come to acquire retrospective meaning, force and significance for her.

What do imaginative writers know?

In his *Studies in Hysteria*, Freud (1895) is famously concerned by the way his psychoanalytic case histories appear to lack 'the serious stamp of science'. '[L]ocal diagnosis and electrical reactions lead nowhere in the history of hysteria', he writes, going on to propose:

> a detailed description of mental processes such as we are accustomed to find in the works of imaginative writers enables me, with the use of a few psychological formulas, to obtain at least some kind of insight into the course of that affliction. Case histories of this kind are intended to be judged like psychiatric ones.
>
> (p. 160)

For Freud, then, it seems that imaginative writers have access to a particular kind of knowledge that is lacking in the more scientific practice of 'local diagnosis'. More puzzlingly, however, is how the kind of 'detailed description' of psychological processes Freud offers in his case histories – detail akin to that offered by 'imaginative writers' – seems to be dismayingly at odds with the kind of detail he thinks is characteristic of a scientific treatise or academic paper. By telling us that his case histories should be evaluated in the same way as a standard scientific report, Freud exposes the competing epistemologies at stake here. There is the kind of knowledge conveyed by the traditional psychiatric or medical article: typically, for Freud, the valid, reliable and replicable kind that bears 'the serious stamp of science'; and there is the kind of knowledge that is conveyed by a gripping *story*: typically the kind that is capable of illuminating something of a particular person's unique experience and manner of psychological suffering. For Freud, then, the psychoanalytic case history emerges as a contested narrative genre, one in which he is always trying to work out where his loyalties lie.

Hadley's short story belongs to a narrative genre that is no less contested than that of the case history; indeed, haggling over 'what makes a short story short' (Friedman, 1958) has been an intermittent topic of debate within literary theory for some time now. Rather than attempting to resolve these long-standing taxonomic disputes, I want to suggest it might be more fruitful to sustain them; not the least because I suspect Hadley's dense, highly-wrought and artful tale of Jane has much to tell us about the kind of knowledge that Freud thought imaginative writers might bring to bear on his psychoanalytic case histories. We might want to remember that literary fiction, as much as psychoanalysis, is intimately concerned with the nature of the self, the nature of human experience. It is interested as much with the subject-matter or content of particular events or experiences, as with the self who undergoes such experiences. But what exactly do we mean by experience? What is the difference between experience and awareness, say, or mere sentience? Walsh (1969) draws on Dewey's (1934) *Art as Experience* to make a distinction between the general flow of experience in life, something that we might think of simply as awareness of what is happening to us, and that which seems to stand out as 'an experience'. When we have 'an experience', we are not simply aware, for example, of being lonely or sad; we are aware of *being* aware. There is a self-reflexive quality to our awareness, allowing us to reflect, think about and *know* that we are experiencing loneliness or sadness. The duality of a self that both experiences something and is also aware of its own experiencing is what allows us to notice and reflect on the quality and character of our experience: to realise what our experience is *like*. Nussbaum (1990) goes on to propose reflection as an important counterweight to the pain and suffering evoked by the cataleptic impression. 'Reflection', she writes, 'permits the critical assessment of impressions, their linking into an overall pattern, their classification and reclassification' (p. 273). So mere experience is not enough; we cannot subsist on cataleptic impressions alone. Like the adult Jane, we will need to assimilate our experience by reflecting on our suffering, getting to grips not only with what it is like, its phenomenology as it were, but also by bearing witness to its effects and consequences in our lives.

Jane, as we have seen, has certainly been made aware of something. She has experienced, recognised, been brought face-to-face with her sexual desire and its betrayal. But could we say that she has had 'an experience'? What could we say she *knows*? As we have seen, without reflection mere experience, however powerful, cannot come to anything. In the last troubling few lines of Hadley's story, we learn that Daniel, by now a successful lawyer as well as a good husband and father, has *no memory at all* of Jane. 'Even if by some miracle he ever met her, and she recognised him and told him the whole story (which she would never do), it wouldn't bring anything back. [...] He's had too much happiness in his life since, too much experience; [...] It's all just gone' (pp. 28–9). Paradoxically, then, a life like Daniel's in which there is 'too much happiness [...] too much experience' appears to incur as little reflection as does Jane's life of 'heavy, patient sorrows'. Yet it is only suffering that *can* incur reflection; for, as Nussbaum (1990) reminds us, suffering is constituted by a 'mark or impress' engraved upon the soul. In the absence of suffering there is no 'mark or impress' to reflect upon: 'it's all just gone'. As Hadley tells us, Daniel 'lost that fine tuning' (p. 29) that would have enabled him, in adulthood, to reflect on his memories and come to know the meaning of his brief encounter with Jane.

Let us return to the question of why Freud seems to oppose the 'work of imaginative writers' with the work of those who write scientific reports or theoretical treatises. In reading fiction, says Walsh (1969), we acquire 'knowledge in the form of realization; the realization of what anything might come to as a form of lived experience' (p. 136). To 'realize' of course, means to make something real, to bring it into existence; and so 'the realization of what anything might come to as a form of lived experience' might suggest not only that reading fiction is itself a form of 'lived experience', but that this 'lived experience' has the capacity to bring into existence a kind of knowing that is more real, more immediate, more vivid and more personal than cognitive or propositional knowing. This is not the kind of knowledge, implies Hadley, that we any more than Jane can acquire in biology, history or art lessons; nor is it the kind of knowledge that will get us, or Jane's brother Robin, into university. It is the kind of knowledge that accrues from *living through an experience*: it shows us, not what something *is*, or what something *does*, but rather *what something is like*.

We might think of psychoanalysis, like fiction, as pre-eminently a practice through which we acquire knowledge of *what suffering is like* 'in the form of realization'. But like Jane, we cannot 'realize' this kind of knowledge by ourselves, by sitting alone to reflect on our pain. Our knowledge will not arrive by way of isolated thought, by 'detached, unemotional, exact intellectual scrutiny'; we need someone else to help us make this kind of knowing *real*: to bring it into existence. It is surely no coincidence, then, that Hadley introduces a counsellor into her tale for this latter purpose. For if we take the liberty of substituting a psychoanalyst for Hadley's counsellor, we can see that psychoanalytic work does not only enable us to reflect on our experiences; rather, within the fiction that is the transference, something becomes real 'as a form of lived experience'. Unconscious feelings that are derived from our early childhood relationships come to be located within the therapeutic relationship where they are permitted their fullest emotional expression and impact. Both patient and analyst can get to know *what they are like*. What was felt 'there and then' early on in life comes to be experienced and recognised 'here and now' with the analyst, often accompanied by considerable pain and suffering. In time, such feelings and the therapeutic relationship within which they emerge will become available for shared reflection and interpretation: something that permits the 'fine-tuning' of experience or, to return to Nussbaum (1990), 'the critical assessment of impressions, their linking into an overall pattern, their classification and reclassification' (p. 273). In this way, psychoanalysis can be understood as a method aimed principally at evoking – and subsequently reflecting on – cataleptic impressions: powerful emotional experiences which, through their painfully intense immediacy, are capable of cutting through our defensive intellectual habits to promote knowledge of unconscious feelings, motives and wishes.

Of course, psychoanalysis, like fiction, also has the capacity to amplify emotional experience, slowing it down to capture, illuminate and reflect on it in ways that are not, or not easily, available in the hurly-burly of real life. This allows us to imagine, describe and become aware of things with far more precision, detail and nuance than we might otherwise be capable of. At the same time, psychoanalysis, like fiction, has the potential considerably to expand on the possibilities in experience that might become available for realisation. By evoking complex unconscious material such as dreams, fantasies and associations in our patients, we as therapists, like readers of fiction, may come to vastly extend, amplify and elaborate our capacity to know *what something is like* through imaginative participation and review. Like Jane, our new knowledge – we might call it countertransference – may even on occasion fill us up, 'not in the form of thoughts but as sensations, overwhelming'. But significantly, our knowledge tends not to be obtained through the 'detached, unemotional, exact intellectual scrutiny of one's condition', as Nussbaum suggests, but rather will accrue within and through a relationship of trust in which intense emotional experiences together with their effects and consequences can be fully felt, acknowledged, reflected on and assimilated.

Perhaps we are in a slightly better position now to understand why Freud hoped this kind of knowledge might best be elucidated via his psychoanalytic case histories rather than via presentation of a scientific report. Getting to know *what something is like* appears to require a medium that itself evokes the phenomenology of the subject's unique experience. Through the tragedy of Jane, Hadley not only *tells* us about the importance of coming to know 'what something is like', she *recruits* us, as readers, into this form of knowing as well. When we become active participants in the story by engaging in an empathic relationship with Jane, we not only come to know what her suffering is 'like' through vicarious identification, we come to know something about our own suffering. And by reflecting on the possible consequences and effects of Jane's suffering along with her counsellor, we also come to reflect on the possible consequences and effects of our own. The capacity of a story to mime the unfolding of experience, as well as to reflect on its effects, permits the reader to know 'what something is like' in a way that is simply unavailable to non-narrative, scientific or academic texts.

But how does the story that is a case history recruit its reader into this particular form of knowing? With what confidence can we claim that the account presented via the medium of a psychoanalytic case history helps us to know what the subject's experience is really 'like'? We would be wise to hesitate before too readily making any such assumption, particularly when we observe the epistemological tensions emerging from the case history's commitment to the texture and particularity of the individual alongside its loyalty to the generalisability and replicability of the knowledge that is thereby obtained. So I want to develop the discussion here by deploying Hadley's tale to help us understand the particular mode of inquiry that Freud uses in psychoanalytic work; for as we shall see, this has implications for understanding the limitations of the case history as a medium that aims to represent the subject in its totality.

An Abduction

Let us recall that the kind of knowledge we accrue by living through an experience is not, as Hadley implies, the kind that can be reduced to a proposition or an argument. It is not universal and generalisable, but rather unique and specific. It is clear that the counsellor, secretly bored by Jane's 'lack of imagination' (p. 27), only starts to prick up her ears when she hears about her fantasy: one that connects Jane to a particular set of feelings tied to a specific memory in the context of a unique set of circumstances. Jane's suffering, Hadley tells us, is 'not like anyone else's' (p. 25). It is distinctive, singular, never to be repeated. It is rooted in what we might call an epistemology of the particular.

Drawing on the work of the cultural historian Carlo Ginzberg, Cave (1988) argues that the classic recognition scene is linked to a method of inquiry that can be traced back to the ancient practices of hunters and diviners. It is a method based on the analysis of particular signs or individual traces such as animal tracks, marks and droppings, by which means hunters were able to reconstruct the likely presence of prey from a sequence of apparently unconnected signs and traces. Linking this early form of knowledge acquisition to the work of professionals as disparate as palaeontologists, historians, detectives and doctors, Cave (1988) goes on to argue:

> the sign of recognition in drama and narrative fiction belongs [...] to the same mode of knowledge as the signature, the clue, the fingerprint or footprint and all other tracks and traces that enable an individual to be identified, a criminal to be caught, a hidden event or state of affairs to be reconstructed.
>
> (p. 250)

This method of inquiry proceeds, like the fairy tale trail of breadcrumbs, by a logic of association. It weaves together a number of puzzlingly disparate pieces of information via an initial, explanatory hypothesis that provides a possible narrative thread. Perhaps this is a mode of knowledge that belongs to psychoanalysis too, as Ginzberg himself suggests, since psychoanalysis is concerned with identifying unconscious or repressed knowledge via disconnected signs or hints concealed within the patient's symptoms, slips of the tongue, dreams and forgotten memories. Freud's logic of (free) association is one that patiently tracks the patient's words, the 'detailed descriptions of mental processes' within which lie fragments of a lost personal experience.

This is a method of inquiry that lies very close to the initial, creative stages of scientific inquiry that the American philosopher of science Charles Peirce called abduction. This kind of abduction – not quite the one we might understand from the title of Hadley's story – is a form of inference that Peirce argues is different from either induction or deduction. Induction involves inferring an explanation or theory from a series of observations, whilst deduction involves predicting the consequences of a particular theory or hypothesis through further testing. Abduction, however, is rather different. It is concerned with only the very preliminary stages of an hypothesis: with finding the simplest and most likely explanation for an incomplete set of observations. It is constituted by 'studying the facts and devising a theory to explain them' (Peirce, 1903, p. 145). Significantly, it is concerned with theorising about unexpected events whose hidden causes may be remote in time and which can be accessed only through their effects; and it may involve an 'instant of surprise', suggests Peirce (p. 154), as old assumptions and expectations are ruptured by the introduction of something new and different. In the same way, Freud (1915) argues for the interruptive force of an unconscious whose existence can only be presupposed on the basis of actions that cannot be explained in any other way. '[O]ur most personal daily experience', he writes,

> acquaints us with ideas that come into our head we do not know where from, and intellectual conclusions arrived at we do not know how. All these conscious acts remain disconnected and unintelligible if we insist upon claiming that every mental act that occurs in us must also necessarily be experienced us through consciousness; on the other hand, they fall into a demonstrable connection if we interpolate between them the unconscious acts that we have inferred.
>
> (p. 167).

This is not the place and nor am I qualified to develop a philosophical treatise on abductive reasoning. But it seems an unlikely coincidence that Hadley has named her story *An Abduction*; and as readers we are surely justified in holding her to a particular and, I suspect, distinctly playful choice of title. After all,

Jane's tale could as well have been called *A Seduction*; but Hadley seems less concerned with the fact of 15-year-old Jane's sexual initiation than with wanting us to be alive to the kind of knowledge that fiction delivers: sensitive to a scene of recognition or anagnorisis that constitutes the very paradigm of narrative and, I want to suggest, of psychoanalysis too. For like the psychoanalyst, the reader of Hadley's tale proceeds by following the hidden signs, the unique mark or impress of cataleptic suffering that lies concealed under the 'flat, bland surface' of the text. If we read these signs carefully, we may come to know something of what Jane's particular, unique experience is like; and if we are interested, as was Freud (1895), in a 'detailed description of mental processes' (p. 165), we may also be able to infer along with her counsellor how the events of a lost weekend one hot summer holiday long ago have come unconsciously to shape and perhaps limit Jane's life. In accompanying Jane on her journey from innocence to experience, we too may come to infer, know and understand something about the unconscious currents tugging beneath the surface of our own lives.

The kind of knowledge that emerges from both fiction and psychoanalysis is, I suggest, a particular and intimate form of knowing that may deeply in-form, or shape, our experience of life. It is the kind of knowledge that we are unlikely to acquire in the classroom; and even a professional clinical training does not guarantee it for it is ineluctably bound up with suffering. It is characterised by a commitment to the particularity, distinctiveness and idiosyncrasy of individual experience that is irreducible to universal principles or generalisable laws. Like the patient's free-associations in psychoanalysis, like the fantasy that Jane recounts to her counsellor, this kind of knowledge is contingent and unrepeatable, emerging from causes that are utterly singular, deeply individual and often unconscious. How then, can we judge its significance? Certainly, what Jane knows – what she has learned from her brief sexual encounter – appears to come to nothing. Hadley makes it clear that Jane's adult life is simple, bland and rather unfulfilled and that the lessons so painfully acquired as a naïve 15-year-old are not put to use in any obvious way. Perhaps, though, we might allow for the possibility that Jane's knowledge will remain hidden away within her as a superbly charged, concentrated nugget of life, a kind of radioactive treasure (Hadley, personal communication, 2019) that accrues significance, force and intensity over time, privately nourishing her dreams and imagination.

To return to the contested epistemological status of the psychoanalytic case history, we can see how this focus on particularity creates an uncomfortable dilemma for Freud. It as if his desire as an imaginative writer-analyst to provide vivid 'detailed descriptions' of a life in all its privacy, specificity and idiosyncrasy is always at cross-purposes with his desire as a scientist to situate the telling of that life within the public domain. To thicken the problem a little further, we can see that the scientific knowledge claims made on behalf of the psychoanalytic case history are significantly undermined by its concern not simply with the unique experience of the patient, but with an experience that emerges as a consequence of the transferential and countertransferential cross-currents swirling between *both* the patient and the analyst working together at a particular time: 'a picture of the exposed and entangled state', as Henry James (1934) puts it, that interrupts and vexes any attempt to place individual patients into universal categories or classes, to render them into generalisable 'cases'. If we further attempt to distinguish between the psychoanalyst-writer who presents herself as author of the case history and the psychoanalyst-writer who stories herself and her patient as characters within the narrative (Ogden, 2005), we can also see how these entanglements and identifications only tend to proliferate. Indeed, by now it is clear the supposed uniqueness of the case history has given way to a paradoxical and dizzying multiplicity entailing considerable ambiguity about exactly what or who is the subject of the case in question. It is hardly surprising, then, that Freud's story-telling skills should inevitably prompt awkward questions for him – and us – about whether and to what extent the narrative appeal and 'thick description' (Geertz, 1973) of his psychoanalytic case histories could ever be raised to the level of a scientifically valid and replicable generalisation.

Unlike Freud, Hadley does not need to establish any evidence that might confirm a theory, a general law or an abstract principle. She is not making any claims to scientific validity; and she does not have to be concerned, at least in the way that Freud (1895) was to become concerned in his case history of Katharina, with issues of confidentiality and anonymity. She is simply – or, as it turns out, not so simply – writing a short story. But as we have seen, Hadley's concern with illuminating the significance of the small event, her interest in rendering the tiny detail of Jane's Peter Pan collar or a dusty footprint in the driveway, reveals more than a passing affinity with the kind of detail that preoccupies the writer of the psychoanalytic case history. Yet Freud (1905) seems to fret at the prospect of his case histories being tarred with a literary brush. In his tale of Dora in 'Fragment of an Analysis of a Case of Hysteria' he writes: 'there are many physicians who, (revolting though it may seem), choose to read a case history of this kind not as a contribution to the psychopathology of the neuroses but as a roman à clef designed for their private delectation' (p. 9). A *roman à clef* is a novel about real events and people disguised as fiction; and so perhaps it is understandable, given his newly-minted approach to psychological treatment, that Freud wants to establish from the outset a firm claim to the scientific rather than literary status of his case histories. But Freud's very insistence here might alert us to a certain ambivalence about what he considers to be the evidence for such a claim: 'the record is not absolutely – phonographically – exact', he cautions, 'but it can claim to a high degree of trustworthiness. Nothing of any importance has been altered in it except in some places the order in which the explanations are given; and this has been done for the sake of presenting the case in a more connected form' (p. 10). In this surge of qualifications and disclaimers, Freud reveals himself to be not a little ill at ease with the way his case studies are so evidently, as Marcus (1976) points out, 'abridged, edited, synthesized and constructed from the very outset' (p. 405). His provisos merely beg the question of how 'exact' a report of psychoanalytic work really has to be before its credentials can be considered 'trustworthy'. For if the case history, like a work of fiction, conveys 'knowledge in the form of realization', if it aims to demonstrate not just what psychoanalytic work *is*, nor what it *does*, but rather what psychoanalytic work is *like*, then it is a genre whose form will surely need to correspond to the narrative account of the patient whose unconscious ensures she does not know what it is she speaks. It will necessarily fail to provide an 'absolutely – phonographically – exact' representation of the subject in its totality. In this sense, trustworthiness might be less about trying to capture an 'exact' record of a therapeutic session, whatever that might mean, and more about fidelity to a psychoanalytic theory of language that governs and delimits the psychoanalyst-author no less than her patient. So perhaps we need to hold lightly the distinction between science and stories that Freud struggles to maintain; not only because of the rhetorical and representational strategies deployed in the psychoanalytic case history (Mulligan, 2017), but also because its very inexactitude mimes the ineluctable limits to self-knowledge of the subject who emerges in the telling of herself within a psychoanalysis. But I see that I am at the point of over-reaching myself here; the pursuit of coherent narratives within psychoanalytic work and the fabular basis of a fragmented, partial self speak to broader concerns than I have space for in this chapter. In Chapter 6, I will attempt to explore in greater detail the way psychoanalysis disrupts conventional ways of narrating a life, drawing on the short story as possible literary model for the subject.

If, for some, Freud's case histories read like fiction, perhaps Hadley's *An Abduction* could be said by a reverse logic to read like a case history. 'If I can get to the heart of Dublin', claims James Joyce (Ellman, 1959) of his novel *Ulysses*, 'I can get to the heart of all the cities in the world' (p. 520). So by way of concluding we might ask what getting to the heart of Jane tells us about all the other Janes in the world. What can the test or representative case, whether in the form of a short story or a psychoanalytic case history, tell us about the lives of everyone else? 'If *p*, then what?' as Forrester (1996) puts it, rather more pithily. Can we, as psychotherapists, learn as much from the fiction of Hadley as we can from the case histories of Freud? For just as Freud wanted to find something in the singularity and distinctiveness of his psychoanalytic case histories that could answer to a more general frame of reference, so too Hadley is concerned to find something within the particularity of her tale that speaks to us all: that has the power, as Nussbaum (1990) would have it, to 'drag us to assent' (p. 265). Indeed, in their search for a form of expression that can straddle the incommensurability between the universal and the unique, the standardised and the specific, both Freud and Hadley could be said to interrogate, blur and even surpass the boundaries of their respective literary genres. Theirs is a quest that, if it does nothing else, at least keeps alive and in circulation the tension between what it might mean to know something of an individual – to recognise the particular 'mark or impress' left by their suffering, and to know what this is like – and what it might mean to know something more general, abstract or theoretical about groups of individuals. Iris Murdoch (1954), one of those rare writers capable of turning a hand to both academic treatise and imaginative fiction, throws down the epistemological gauntlet in her characteristically trenchant way: 'The movement away from theory and generality', she announces, 'is the movement towards truth. All theorizing is flight. We must be ruled by the situation itself and this is unutterably particular' (p. 80). In her tale of Jane, Hadley shows us what it is like to be ruled by the situation itself; and by grounding us in her epistemologies of the particular, she reminds us of the fragility of our organised schemes of knowledge, leading us towards emotional truths via wonderfully imagined paths.

Note

1 All references in the text to *An Abduction* are taken from Hadley, T. (2017). *Bad Dreams and Other Stories*. London: Jonathan Cape.

References

Aristotle (2013). *Poetics*. Oxford World's Classics, Oxford University Press.

Boitani, P. (2021). *Anagnorisis: Scenes and Themes of Recognition and Revelation from Western Literature*. Leiden, Netherlands and Boston, MA: Brill.

Cave, T. (1988). *Recognitions. A Study in Poetics*. Oxford: Clarendon Press.

Dewey, J. (1934). *Art as Experience*. New York: Perigee Books, 1980.

Ellman, R. (1959). *James Joyce*. Oxford: Oxford University Press.

Flaubert, G. (1869). *Sentimental Education*. London: Penguin Classics, Revised edition, 2004.

Forrester, J. (1996). If p, then what? Thinking in cases. *History of the Human Sciences*, 9, 3: 1–25.

Freud, S. (1895). *Studies in Hysteria*. London: Penguin, 2004.

Freud, S. (1905). Fragment of an analysis of a case of hysteria (1905 [1901]). In: J. Strachey (ed. and trans.), *The Standard Edition of the Complete Psychological Works of Sigmund Freud*, Vol. 7, pp. 1–122. London: Hogarth. Freud, S. (1915). The unconscious. In: J. Strachey (ed. and trans.), *The Standard Edition of the Complete Psychological Works of Sigmund Freud*, Vol. 14, pp. 159–215. London: Hogarth.

Friedman, N. (1958). What makes a short story short? *Modern Fiction Studies*, 4, 2: 103–17.

Geertz, C. (1973). *The Interpretation of Cultures: Selected Essays*. New York: Basic Books.

Hadley, T. (2017). *Bad Dreams and Other Stories*. London: Jonathan Cape.

Halliwell, S. (1987). *The Poetics of Aristotle*. London: Duckworth.

Hartley, L.P. (1953). *The Go-Between*. London: Penguin Modern Classics, New edition, 2004.

James, H. (1897). *What Maisie Knew*. London: Penguin Classics, Revised edition, 2010.

James, H. (1934). *The Art of the Novel: Critical Prefaces by Henry James*. Chicago and London: University of Chicago Press, 2011.

Marcus, S. (1976). Freud and Dora: story, history, case history. *Psychoanalysis and Contemporary Science*, 5: 389–442.

Mulligan, D. (2017). The storied analyst: desire and persuasion in the clinical vignette. *The Psychoanalytic Quarterly*, 86, 4: 811–833.
Murdoch, I. (1954). *Under The Net*. London: Penguin Books.
Nussbaum, M. (1990). *Love's Knowledge. Essays on Philosophy and Literature*. Oxford: Oxford University Press, pp. 261–285.
Ogden, T. (2005). On psychoanalytic writing. *International Journal of Psycho-Analysis*, 85: 15–29.
Peirce, C. (1903). *Harvard Lectures on 'Pragmatism as a Principle and Method of Right Thinking'*. The Charles S. Peirce Manuscripts.Cambridge, MA: The Houghton Library of Harvard University.
Walsh, D. (1969). *Literature and Knowledge*. Middletown, CT: Wesleyan University Press.

Chapter 5

On food, faith and psychoanalysis
Isak Dinesen's *Babette's Feast*

Introduction

Having reached the age of reason at seven years old, it was time, my mother said, for me to make my First Holy Communion. The nuns who were teaching me at the small Catholic convent girls' school in London where I grew up were excited. 'You are very lucky children', Mother Gabriel announced to the class, her black eyes shining beneath her cream-coloured wimple. 'You are going to receive a gift. The best gift in the world. It's the body of Christ!' I nodded solemnly, along with my friends. I knew all about Holy Communion. Every week for years, I had watched my mother queue during Sunday mass to receive a small wafer from the priest in her outstretched hands. She would stand there, put it in her mouth, cross herself and return back to the pew where I was waiting. Respectfully, I would shift my knees awkwardly to one side to allow her room to pass by and kneel down; and there she would stay on her knees, freshly holy, for the next quarter of an hour or so while I sat, hungry, fidgeting and impatient, waiting for the priest to conclude mass.

The practice session held at school was, truth to tell, a bit of a disappointment. We all trooped down importantly to the little chapel off the hall to walk slowly, one by one, up to a gimlet-eyed Reverend Mother standing by the altar holding a silver cup filled with unblessed communion hosts ('quite all right to use these, girls, they haven't yet been turned into the Lord's body'). When my turn came, I shut my eyes tightly, and proceeded cautiously towards the altar with one hand cupped on top of the other as if playing an ecclesiastical version of Grandmother's Footsteps. I stopped as soon as I heard the words 'the Body of Christ', obediently repeating what Mother Gabriel had told me to say: 'Amen'. I felt a firm pressure in my palm. When I opened my eyes, I saw a small, light, paper-coloured disc in my hand which I gingerly picked up – so light! Was that all? – and put in my mouth. To my dismay, it promptly and firmly stuck to the roof of my mouth; and while my tongue, at first apologetically, then more urgently and finally with distinct alarm attempted to dislodge it, it dissolved into a sticky, glutinous mass only to slide down my throat before I could get back to my seat. Guiltily, I knelt down, glancing surreptitiously at my friends who all appeared to be self-

DOI: 10.4324/9781003325468-6

consciously chewing and swallowing Jesus, sitting back with satisfied smiles on their faces. Clearly, I needed more practice and I resolved to do better next time.

The problem was, as I decided later, it didn't look like a body. Actually, it didn't really look like bread either, resembling more the rice paper that clung to the bottom of the coconut macaroons I was rather fond of. If, as I had been told, it was really the body of Christ – His Real Presence – how could I eat it? Didn't that make me a cannibal? And anyway, what happened once the wafer was in my tummy? How long did it last there? Of course, I knew that I had to fast before taking communion, but what would happen afterwards, when I ate my Zing bar during morning break? It seemed vaguely sacrilegious to eat chocolate on top of the Body of Christ; and besides, there was the complicated and delicate matter of digestion. These were perhaps not quite the sacred mysteries that I was supposed to be contemplating, but they were deeply important matters for my confused seven-year-old self. The puzzling questions remained; but alas, there was no time to work out the answers before the great First Holy Communion Day arrived, and what with the glamour, flowers and crowds at school, the photographs, the proud parents and the delighted nuns, the vexed issue of exactly how something that appeared to be bread could at the same time be something divine, faded into the background.

Perhaps now, as a psychotherapist, it is not surprising that I find myself absorbed by the question of what it might mean for the presence of another to cross the bounds of flesh and take up residence within. By what means does a loved one come to inhabit and inspire us? How does the lost, absent or dead other continue to evoke a sense of loving relationship inside us? How might we come to trust or have faith in this inner presence over time? In psychoanalysis, these are questions that have largely been addressed in terms of identification, that central psychic mechanism through which we unconsciously absorb or incorporate aspects of each other. Theorists from Freud to Laplanche have argued that our subjectivity seems to be predicated on a kind of psychological permeability in which we find ourselves open to the other who lodges within, imprinting upon us a sense of their inner presence. Whilst I have attempted to explore some aspects of this phenomenon in my reading of Kazuo Ishiguro's *Never Let Me Go* in Chapter 1, the extraordinary and constitutive process of psychic ingestion remains to me essentially a mysterious one, and something in this chapter I want to investigate further in my reading of Isak Dinesen's novella *Babette's Feast*. This is one of several short stories she wrote in a collection called *Anecdotes of Destiny*, published at the end of her life in 1958. In a deceptively simple tale, Dinesen adopts explicitly Eucharistic discourse and imagery to convey the connection between eating and faith, exploring via rich use of metaphor the way in which we come to be inhabited and nourished by the other. Indeed, for Dinesen, transubstantiation – that mystical transformation of one substance into another, of bread into the Body of Christ, of food into faith – may be taken as exemplar of what might be called a sacramental imagination, one in which the material world is viewed as both participant in and mediator of the divine.

From the outset, however, it is important to distinguish the term 'sacramental imagination' from the sacraments of ecclesiology, though these may be included within its overall framework. According to the Catholic Church, 'a Sacrament is a visible sign of invisible grace, instituted for our justification' (Catechism of the Council of Trent, 143), something that implies belief in a God of metaphysical dogma. Sacramental imagination, on the other hand, can be thought of as a wider concept encompassing the effort to reach out towards transcendence, to give voice, shape, colour, sound and words to that which exceeds the visible or the material. By illuminating the invisible dimension of the world, in bringing to our attention a vivid awareness of what lies beneath the surface of tangible realities, it is writers and artists who are amongst those best placed to help us move beyond religious doctrine and creed to celebrate, as Kearney (2010) suggests, 'the bread and wine of the everyday' (p. 183). Indeed, by inviting us to be attentive to signs of the divine in the world around us, we might think of the sacramental imagination as something that enables us to experience something 'other' or 'more': a state of mind or psychic register that pierces reality, as it were, allowing us to see the transcendent in the immanent, the infinite in the finite and the sacred in the mundane.

In this chapter, I want to follow Dinesen's sacramental imagination by exploring how her tale of Babette opens up a space in which the passage or assimilation of the other into the self may be illuminated. I suggest that Dinesen's use of food as metaphor persuasively links transubstantiation with the psychoanalytic project by revealing the different ways in which we may receive – or eat – the other, and what these differences might entail for the work of memory and mourning. It is important to note that, like Dinesen, I am not primarily interested in theological argument and dispute. Rather, I am more interested in responding to her tale as a kind of parable, a narrative form indexed by her use of simple, spare language, lack of distracting detail and most of all her directions to the reader to be aware of a more profound significance to the story. Unlike the allegory that guides us towards a specific meaning in the text, the parable merely hints, alludes or gestures towards something. It indicates, rather than designates; its meaning is open, not closed. It invites and provokes curiosity, wonder, thought. The reader is to be teased into making his or her own meaning from it and living accordingly. As Ricoeur (1975) suggests, a parable 'is a fiction capable of redescribing life', where the whole text is 'the bearer of metaphors' whose 'ultimate point [...] is not the reign of God, but the whole of human reality' (p. 89). It is in this light I think we are invited to encounter and enjoy Dinesen's tale, and it is in this light too that I hope to provoke the reader to find something of his or her own within some of the ideas presented in my reading of the story.

Babette's Feast[1]

Dinesen's tale is set in the bleak territory of Jutland in Norway, in the village of Berlevaag where two elderly sisters are living out a simple life in a small

Lutheran community. They are helped in the house by a Parisian maid, Babette, and neighbours assume that it is the sisters' 'piety and kindness of heart' (p. 24) that led them to employ her. We learn that Babette was indeed taken care of by the sisters when she first arrived in Berlevaag some twelve years previously, hungry and frightened, a fugitive from the Paris Communard uprisings of 1871 in which her husband and son were both killed. But the reason for Babette's presence in the house of the two sisters was to be found, Dinesen tells us, 'further back in time and deeper down in the domain of human hearts' (p. 24).

These two sisters, Martine and Philippa, have been brought up by a strict, puritanical father, the Dean of a religious sect who leads his flock in their lives of austere simplicity. Any sign of luxury, worldly comfort or fleshly satisfaction is condemned. Food is sparse, clothes are simple; life consists in good deeds and works of charity. The Dean exerts a strict and uncompromising control over the girls' lives and they in turn are imbued with 'an ideal of heavenly love' (p. 25). They reject the young men of the village rather than allow themselves 'to be touched by the flames of this world' (p. 25). Into this bleak, joyless community Dinesen introduces three strangers. The first is Lorens Loewenhielm, a young officer whose spendthrift ways have resulted in his parents sending him to live with his elderly aunt in Berlevaag for a few weeks. He sees and falls in love with Martine. She reminds him of the 'huldre', a mysterious Norwegian mountain spirit, 'who is so fair that the air round her shines and quivers' (p. 26). He tries but fails to communicate his feelings and in the end despairs of ever removing her from the ascetic life insisted upon by the Dean, her father. He leaves, telling Martine that he has learned that 'Fate is hard, and that in this world there are things which are impossible!' (p. 27). He returns to the world to focus on his career, marries a lady-in-waiting to the Queen, and moves 'with grace and ease' (p. 28) in high circles.

The second stranger to appear is the exotic French opera singer, Achille Papin. Hearing Philippa sing in church, he realises that she has the voice of a great diva and offers to teach her singing. The Dean, reluctant at first to allow this Catholic man access to his daughter, eventually agrees and singing lessons begin. However, one day, when they are singing Mozart's seduction duet from Don Giovanni, Papin gets carried away by the 'heavenly music' (p. 31) and kisses Philippa. '[S]urprised and frightened by something in her own nature' (p. 32), she returns to her father saying that she no longer wishes to learn singing and asks him to dismiss Papin, who makes a precipitate departure from Berlevaag.

Fifteen years later, the Dean is dead and Martine and Philippa have remained at home, continuing their lives of pious self-denial. One stormy night, a knock at the door reveals a wet, famished Babette Hersant, seeking refuge from a shipwreck. She brings with her a letter from Achille Papin, who tells them that Babette has fled her home in Paris, fearing arrest for her role as a 'petroleuse' revolutionary in the Paris Communard uprisings. 'Babette can cook' (p. 34) is the laconic footnote provided at the end of the letter in which

Papin pleads for the sisters to look after Babette. Although the sisters cannot afford to pay Babette, they agree to take her in; and so, finally, it is the third stranger who is the one accepted into the community.

For twelve years Babette looks after the home of Martine and Philippa. Alarmed at the possibility of any untoward French extravagance – and hopeful of converting Babette to the good Lutheran life – the sisters train her in the abstemious ways of the household, teaching her to cook 'split cod and an ale-and-bread soup as well as anybody born and bred in Berlevaag' (p. 36). During these years, we read how the sisters find themselves presiding over their dead father's dwindling flock where 'sad little schisms' (p. 23) increasingly reveal that the Dean's strict moral teachings have failed to engender moral enlightenment in the community. Although the faithful still meet together 'to read and interpret the Word' (p. 24), ancient sins and transgressions are recalled with deep resentment and bitterness, and quarrels flare up which the worried sisters find themselves unable to calm.

But chance intervenes on the occasion of the Dean's hundredth anniversary. Babette, whose friend in Paris has been renewing a lottery ticket every year for her, receives a letter telling her that she has won the *grand prix* of 10,000 francs. As the news gets out, the sisters and the Dean's flock all sadly assume that Babette's riches will mean she will want to return home to Paris. But Babette comes to the sisters with the first request she has ever made in her twelve years of service; she wants to provide a French celebration dinner for the Dean's flock on the occasion of his anniversary. While the sisters protest, Babette insists that she would like to spend her own money on this meal for the sisters and the Dean's followers; and although the sisters at first refuse, shocked at the prospect of anything more than 'a very plain supper with a cup of coffee' (p. 42), she persuades them to grant her wish.

Babette swiftly organises her nephew to travel with her to France to collect the things that she will need for the meal. By the time these arrive and preparations are under way, the sisters realise uneasily that something extraordinary is going on. 'Babette, like the bottled demon of the fairy tale, had swelled and grown to such dimensions that her mistresses felt small before her' (p. 45). Bottles of wine and even a live turtle are brought to the home, and this is so terrifying, so alien, that Philippa hastily convenes a meeting of the faithful fearing their frugal ways are about to be violated. After some sympathetic discussion, the brethren agree that on the day of the meal, they will not discuss the food and drink at all. Indeed, they promise they will not even taste anything, in order to preserve themselves for higher things.

The celebratory evening arrives, and old Mrs Loewenhielm is invited to the dinner along with the few remaining brethren. By chance, General Loewenhielm, her nephew, is visiting for the first time in 30 years, and remembering him the sisters are delighted to invite him to the meal along with his aunt. World weary after a successful military career and a busy time with his wife at Court, we learn that General Loewenhielm now finds himself in low spirits. Pondering whether the world is 'not a moral, but a mystic concern' (p. 52), he muses over his choices in life as he prepares for dinner, and questions whether his younger self who left Martine in Berlevaag all those years ago did the right thing.

Arriving at the house, the visitors and the Dean's flock sit down to a beautifully decorated dinner table. As the wine is served, the brethren remember their vow not to speak about or taste the food. But General Loewenhielm who has been expecting the simple fare he was served on his last visit, is immediately surprised at the 'finest Amontillado I have ever tasted' (pp. 55–6), as well as the magnificent turtle soup. A succession of extraordinary dishes is served – 'Incredible! [...] It is Blinis Demidoff!' (p. 56) – and the General, a man of the world, is increasingly amazed at the quality of the food that is being presented. In the unfolding of a gently comic scene, he cannot understand how his fellow diners are 'all quietly eating their Blinis Demidoff without any sign of either surprise or approval, as if they had been doing so every day for thirty years' (p. 56).

During the meal the guests find themselves gradually opening themselves up to receiving and enjoying the food that Babette provides for them. Despite their vows to the contrary, the ascetic philosophy to which they had agreed to adhere is all but dismissed: 'It was, they realized, when man has not only altogether forgotten but has firmly renounced all ideas of food and drink that he eats and drinks in the right spirit' (p. 58). The transformative process occurring during this rapturous eating is beautifully conveyed not only by the way the sophisticated General speaks to the other guests 'in a manner so new to himself and so strangely moving that after the first sentence he had to make pause' (p. 60), but also by the inexperienced Brethren's surrender to the hitherto unsuspected delights of haute cuisine:

> This time the Brothers and Sisters knew that what they were given to drink was not wine, for it sparkled. It must be some kind of lemonade. The lemonade agreed with their exalted state of mind and seemed to lift them off the ground, into a higher and purer sphere.
>
> (p. 57)

But when *Cailles en sarcophages*, an exotic dish of quails in pastry is served, the General at once recognises the signature dish of the chef at the Café Anglais in Paris, where he used to dine with his military friends. He remembers that this chef, 'known all over Paris as the greatest culinary genius of the age' (p. 58) was a woman, and one whom his friend claimed turned 'dinner at the Café Anglais into a kind of love affair [...] in which one no longer distinguishes between bodily and spiritual appetite or satiety' (p. 58). Indeed, by the end of the meal, not only have the frugal Brethren come to acquire an appreciation of the sensual, worldly pleasures they have previously rejected, but General Loewenhielm himself has arrived at an understanding of the spiritual meaning that has hitherto evaded him in life. The joyous reconciliation of the Brethren with each other and the physical world is matched by

General Loewenhielm's peaceful reconciliation with the spiritual dimension in himself:

> Grace, brothers, makes no conditions and singles out none of us in particular; grace takes us all to its bosom and proclaims general amnesty. See! That which we have chosen is given us, and that which we have refused is, also and at the same time, granted us. Ay, that which we have rejected is poured upon us abundantly.
>
> (p. 60)

General Loewenhielm realises that his choices in life have, after all, been made good. He leaves Martine saying 'Every evening I shall sit down, if not in the flesh, which means nothing, but in spirit which is all, to dine with you [...] For tonight I have learned, dear sister, that in the world, anything is possible' (p. 62). The community, too, realises that the 'infinite grace of which General Loewnenhielm had spoken had been allotted to them' (p. 62), and finally, when '[l]ong after midnight the windows of the house shone like gold' (p. 61) they stagger off hand in hand, all bitterness and quarrels forgotten, laughing and singing all the way back home.

In the aftermath of the feast, the sisters return to the kitchen to thank Babette, only to realise that it was she who was the chef at the Café Anglais. The sisters assume that Babette will now be returning to Paris and are horrified to hear that she has no more money; she has spent her entire fortune of 10,000 francs on the celebration dinner. Philippa sees Babette's generosity as an act of self-sacrifice, but Babette responds by saying that she has done it for her own sake; and that creating the dinner was necessary in order to fulfil her destiny as a great artist.

Isak Dinesen

Dinesen, while raised a Unitarian, never claimed to be a Christian and throughout her life was deeply suspicious of what she regarded as Christian dualism. Nevertheless, while she was writing *Babette's Feast* she was heavily immersed in a study of Christian theology and hosted several 'theological dinners' to which she invited a Roman Catholic priest, a Lutheran pastor and other Christian church authorities. Lane (1999), in discussing these dinners, suggests that Dinesen 'was obviously influenced by the conversation, especially that of the sacramentalist Catholic priest' (p. 22); and indeed various critics and writers have offered a convincing allegorical reading of *Babette's Feast* (e.g. Beck, 1998; Mullins, 2009; Wright, 1997), viewing elements of the story such as Babette's sacrifice, the twelve dinner guests and the transformative effects of the sacrificial meal on the community as a reflection of the Last Supper and Christ's crucifixion. However, Dinesen's interest in Catholic imagery and aesthetics goes far beyond the merely allegorical. She introduces us to the enigmatic stranger, the servant, who comes to town tasked with introducing life, faith and change into the ageing, fractious, Lutheran community. Perhaps, as Levinas (1969) has intimated, the encounter with the figure of the Stranger is always sacred in that he or she embodies something more, something different; something surplus to that which we can contain within ourselves. It is our response to the Stranger, the hospitality we are willing to extend to the foreigner, the Other,[2] that determines our ability to host and house the divine within ourselves. Babette, the bottled demon of the fairy tale, the genie who arrives on the sisters' doorstep and stays for twelve years, not only introduces something new, Catholic and Southern into the cold, bleak Protestant North; she also introduces the sisters and the community to something strange and new within their own natures. In this sense, Babette's enigmatic presence may be seen as a wider parable for how we come to receive or incorporate the divine within ourselves: how we can allow it to inhabit us in ways that are creative or transformative, in ways that might make good our losses. Dinesen draws on the rich metaphor of food to convey the difference between a dogmatic faith that, like the sisters' tasteless split cod and ale-and-bread soup, is swallowed whole by the Dean's flock who consistently refuse to acknowledge the presence of the divine in 'the pleasures of the world'; and a sacramental view of life that instead grasps the divine in each moment, a faith that is 'chewed over', and savoured like the famous dish of *Cailles en sarcophages* that Babette presents to her amazed dinner guests. Indeed, the centre-piece celebratory meal is one that places loss at the heart of the story; for this is a community that has in every sense lost its way, mired in 'querulous and quarrelsome' (p. 23) relationships since the loss of its beloved founding father the Dean. This constitutes the backdrop to the sorrow with which the main characters are struggling: the regret that is experienced by the General at his youthful decision to leave Martine; Philippa's wistfulness at the loss of her promising singing career; and, most of all, Babette's unspoken grief at being forced to leave her home, her murdered husband and son and her artistic vocation as a chef. These heartaches and losses underpin and drive Babette's culinary artistry as she seeks to heal the community by preparing, cooking and serving a meal of which she herself is the main constituent.

I want to suggest that Dinesen's tale of eating and loss allows us to freshly explore some familiar psychoanalytic territory, including the concepts of identification, introjection and mourning. At this point, then, we will turn to the ideas of Freud, Abraham and Torok, and Kristeva before attempting to develop an understanding of the central themes of transformation and transubstantiation that Dinesen elaborates in her story of Babette. As we shall see, these are themes whose significance extends far beyond the abstract or theoretical, instead reaching deep into the ethics of the psychoanalytic encounter itself.

Eating and psychoanalysis

Eating, of course, has always occupied a privileged place in psychoanalytic theory. From the ferocity of Freud's oral drives, through Klein's dark infantile fantasies of biting, sucking and spitting to Winnicott's more benign cycles of appetite, greed, destruction and concern, psychoanalysis has always invoked the metaphor of consumption to articulate the various ways in which we attempt to take in something from outside and install it within the self. We seem to be born strangely porous, with a capacity to receive, ingest and somehow retain the presence, the 'feel', of those we love within. As Meghan O'Rourke (2012) says in her biography *The Long Goodbye*: 'The people we most love do become a physical part of us, ingrained in our synapses in the pathways where memories are created'. Freud was always interested in the mysterious way in which the other becomes installed within the self, incarnate within the psyche. In 1917, he had suggested how, in melancholia, the ego identifies with the lost object, subsuming it within the ego as a means of refusing to mourn its loss. By 1923, however, he saw this psychic absorption of the other into the ego as a more central feature of personality development: 'the character of the ego', he writes, 'is a precipitate of abandoned object cathexes [...] it contains the history of those object choices' (p. 29). In all these consummatory versions of personality development, identification seems to be a means of ensuring a kind of inner fidelity that indexes the ego's allegiance to the presence of the lost, loved other within.

Following Freud's distinction between mourning and melancholia, Abraham and Torok (1994) argue that the fantasy of introducing all or part of the love object into the body as a means of retaining it is a way of effecting psychic transformation 'through magic' (p. 126). 'So in order not to have to "swallow" a loss', they write, 'we fantasize swallowing (or having swallowed) that which has been lost, as if it were some kind of thing' (p. 126). Incorporation thus attempts a magical cure for loss by ingesting the lost object as if it were food. In this moment of psychic absorption, 'we refuse to mourn and ... we shun the consequences of mourning even though our psyche is fully bereaved' (p. 127). The loss is thus buried alive, they suggest, concealed in a kind of 'intrapsychic crypt' within the ego that protects the loss from ever being assimilated and spoken. In this way, a loss can itself go missing, hidden within an absence in which the individual may insist that, to all intents and purposes, he or she had lost nothing. In this situation 'one feels justified', says Freud (1917), 'in maintaining the belief that a loss [...] has occurred, but one cannot see clearly what it is that has been lost, and it is all the more reasonable to suppose that the patient cannot consciously perceive what he has lost either' (p. 245).

Incorporation means that the subject in fantasy gulps down and swallows all or part of a person, instead of the more laborious, slow and incremental process of feeding on words that might speak to his or her absence. In the long-term project of introjection or mourning that Abraham and Torok

(1994) argue originates in infancy, 'words replace the mother's presence [...] the absence of objects and the empty mouth are transformed into words; at last, even the experiences related to words are converted into other words' (p. 128). Perhaps our earliest experiences of feeding, handling and physical care mean that we are born into a kind of faith in the physical presence, the body of the other who underwrites our existence, who guarantees the life of desire. And it is through faith in the presence of the body that we come to have faith in the presence of words, symbols that give shape to, and make up for, the loved person's physical absence.

Esther Rashkin (2008) has drawn on Abraham and Torok's (1994) ideas, arguing convincingly that the meal Babette serves starts the process of mourning in the community by converting the community's loss and grief following the death of the Dean into language through the form of communion with bereaved others. However, here I want to suggest that the losses to which Rashkin draws attention are emblematic of a yet more profound loss within the community: 'It was as if the fine and lovable vigor of their father's personality had been evaporating', says Dinesen of Martine and Philippa, 'the way Hoffmann's anodyne will evaporate when left on the shelf in a bottle without a cork' (p. 39). It is surely not coincidental here that 'Hoffman's anodyne' is otherwise known as a compound of ether, a substance that in ancient mythology was considered to be the pure essence breathed by the gods. So Dinesen is perhaps hinting here at a slipping away of divine inspiration or grace that leaves the Brothers and Sisters of Berlevaag 'running astray' like 'unshepherded sheep' (p. 39).

In order to develop my thoughts about the spiritual loss to which Dinesen alludes, I want to turn to the writing of Julia Kristeva whose preoccupation with Catholic symbolism and imagery, in particular her interest in the significance of hosting the Stranger, the foreigner within, aligns her closely – to my mind at least – with Dinesen's sacramental imagination. In her break with Lacan, Kristeva has always sought to emphasise the child's earliest relation to the maternal body, and the importance of the semiotic drives underlying, guaranteeing and disrupting the Symbolic order of language and the Law of the Father. In amplifying the traditional theories of identification mentioned above, Kristeva (1990) argues that the object we incorporate in primary narcissism is not simply the fantasy of fusion with the maternal body; it is rather a metaphorical object, one that is inclusive of the imaginary father towards whom the child turns in order to separate from the maternal body and become a speaking subject. It is as if, in the moment of identification, the child consumes something else alongside the fantasy of the maternal body: there is a simultaneous identification with Freud's (1923) father of 'personal prehistory' (p. 31) who is the object of the mother's love; a love that is communicated through language and which underpins the not-yet-speaking subject. 'This movement', claims O'Grady (1997), 'is not one of possession or need ... but a movement toward identification with a loved other. It is not a motion to '*have*' but a gesture toward '*being like*' (*être-comme*), that is, a '*metaphoric* identification' (p. 102). It is this metaphoric identification with the father-in-the-mother – or what is 'other' or different within the maternal body – that allows the child to begin imaginatively to identify with what is 'other' or different within itself. What we might call a logic of identification permits the developing child to have confidence – faith – in the possibility of one thing standing in for another: to believe and take comfort in the capacity of words to name, to 'stand in for', that which has been lost.

Psychoanalysis and transubstantiation

The word metaphor means a 'carrying over', etymologically linked to the Greek *meta*, which means over or across and *pherein*, to carry or bear, from which we derive the word 'fertile'. Metaphors, suggests Aristotle in his *Poetics*, rely on our capacity to find similarities between two disparate things. Like words themselves that carry us across the gap to the things they signify, metaphors too ferry us across and between alterity towards something else, something beyond the literal words themselves. Metaphor thus stretches the signifying system in a way that forces it to carry more than it can bear. It is emblematic of the mind's fertility: language at its most generative and creative. Alain Robbe-Grillet (1965) predicts suggestively that '[i]f you begin by believing in metaphor, you will end by believing in God' (p. 78).

This notion of 'carrying over' or across is thus crucial for Kristeva, for whom metaphor is not simply a linguistic turn but rather a dynamic psychic transaction at the heart of subjectivity and intersubjectivity. Metaphors, for Kristeva, are emblematic of what destabilises, disrupts and dissolves the unified subject. The divided speaking subject is radically transformed in the process of metaphorical identification, as borders, limits and boundaries between signifiers blur, carrying the subject across and back to that which is sacred or divine within. Indeed, O'Grady (1997) goes on to point out that for Kristeva, metaphor may be understood as the unconscious linguistic pursuit of the ineffable, sublime Other, an attempt by the subject to grasp that which is lost, absent and unnameable within the self. In her essay on 'Identification and the real' (1990), Kristeva suggests that the Eucharistic meal is 'the perfect enactment of the metaphorical process' (p. 172), entailing precisely this kind of 'blurring' in which the actual absorption of the body of Christ into the subject fuses the physical/food with the psychic/Word. For Kristeva, then, the Eucharistic rite enacts the passage of internal strangeness or otherness at the heart of each of us where the physical and the psychic are welded together. Here, in this moment of transubstantiation, is the subject's opportunity for transformation and metamorphosis.

Like Dinesen, Kristeva makes no claim to be Catholic, merely drawing on Catholic imagery and discourse to illuminate the subjective significance of hosting the stranger, the foreigner within. 'I speak of religions', she claims in an interview with Clark and Hulley (1990), 'because the question of the other is fundamentally, I think, a religious question' (p. 164). However, it is inevitable that both Dinesen and Kristeva's use of the Eucharist will raise important differences between the Catholic and the Protestant understanding of the term. In Catholicism, according to the Council of Trent (1551), transubstantiation is a miraculous process of consecration in which the 'substance' of bread and wine is converted into the 'substance' of the body and blood of Christ. The appearance, or 'species' of the bread and wine remain the same, while the substance – the 'breadness' of the bread, for example – is transformed into the body and blood of Christ. Christ's Real Presence is said to be contained in the elements of the bread and wine that have been transubstantiated. In Protestantism, there are a variety of views on the Eucharist, or communion as it is more often called, depending on the particular denomination. However, most Protestants regard communion as a symbolic act commemorating the Last Supper, Christ's Passion and His promise of redemption.

This ontological distinction lies at the heart of *Babette's Feast*, in which a dinner is prepared to remember the loss of the Dean. When the Catholic Babette asks Martine and Philippa if she can cook a 'real French dinner' for the Dean's 100th anniversary, the sisters are horrified. 'The ladies had not intended to have any dinner at all' we are told. 'A very plain supper with a cup of coffee was the most sumptuous meal to which they had ever asked any guest to sit down' (p. 42). When the time comes for the party, the sisters' 'little preparations' (p. 48) suggest that the meal is expected to be merely commemorative, an opportunity to 'put on their old black best frocks and their confirmation gold crosses' (p. 49) and, along with their fellow Brothers and Sisters, sing one of the Dean's favourite hymns. However, in Dinesen's version of transubstantiation, 'something has happened', as the poet Mary Oliver (2006) says, to the food and drink. Babette's culinary artistry transforms the food's very 'substance' into something miraculous, something that enables the 'taciturn old people' to receive 'the gift of tongues' (p. 61) and to retrieve the lost feelings of love they had for each other in a way that redeems the community.

That this change is effected by transubstantiation is underlined by Dinesen in a small but telling epilogue where the sisters go to thank Babette after the dinner. Finding her sitting exhausted in the kitchen, Martine privately recalls a tale told to her by her father's friend who had been a missionary in Africa:

> He had saved the life of an old chief's favourite wife, and to show his gratitude the chief had treated him to a rich meal. Only long afterwards the missionary came to learn from his own black servant that what he had partaken of was a small fat grandchild of the chief's, cooked in honour of the great Christian medicine man.
>
> (p. 66)

It is precisely this absorption, this consummation – rather than commemoration – of the other within us that Dinesen, like Kristeva, wants us to understand is the more profound issue at stake. Indeed, just as Christ says in the words of the Gospel of St John (6:56): 'He that eateth my flesh, and drinketh my blood, dwelleth in me, and I in him', this is a consummation that ensures a restoration of the divine within the flesh, and, more importantly for the abstemious Dean's flock, the flesh to the divine. This restoration is gloriously conveyed during Babette's celebratory dinner where the ascetic Brethren move from a position of comically refusing to acknowledge the delicious food and drink to one in which they become joyously able to receive and appreciate it in the right way. 'It was, they realized, when man has not only altogether forgotten but has firmly renounced all ideas of food and drink that he eats and drinks in the right spirit' (p. 58). It is unclear to the participants – and to the reader – whether the miracle of their metamorphosis occurs via their bodily senses or their spirits. Indeed, 'the convives', says Dinesen, 'grew lighter in weight and lighter of heart the more they ate and drank' (pp. 57–8). Body and spirit seem to be interchangeable here; or, rather, the usual distinction between the flesh and the soul, the worldly and the otherworldly, no longer appears relevant. Dinesen's text thus wonderfully hints at a blurring and surpassing of traditional dualisms, a transubstantiation in which 'the Word', as St. John writes (1:14), 'was made Flesh and dwelt among us, full of grace and truth'. 'Of what happened later in the evening nothing definite can here be stated', says Dinesen of the dinner guests. 'They only knew that the rooms had been filled with a heavenly light, as if a number of small halos had blended into one glorious radiance [...] Time itself had merged into eternity' (p. 61). The ecstatic blending of the spiritual and the corporeal here is a kind of reversible fusion 'in which', as General Loewenhielm's friend points out, 'one no longer distinguishes between bodily and spiritual appetite or satiety' (p. 58). It is a transubstantiation that transports the subject, that welds the self to the essence of the other, that ingrains the other within our very synapses. The self is no longer just the self, but is now 'carried over' above and beyond itself, imbued and saturated with the other's presence. And it is not blind belief in the Dean's teaching, but rather a willing receptiveness to the presence of this inner union that ensures, through the General's speech at dinner, the arrival of grace in the community: 'Grace, my friends, demands nothing from us but that we shall await it with confidence and acknowledge it in gratitude [...] for mercy and truth have met together and righteousness and bliss have kissed one another' (pp. 60–1). Indeed, the Danish word for grace is *nade*, linked via the German term *gnade* to the notion of descent, as in the image of the sun's descent in the sky (Braune, 2007); and so grace carries the connotation of an ineffable love descending from the heights to touch the horizon of our world, bringing God closer to man. The General's speech thus sets the seal on the restoration of grace within the community; a grace that brings both the 'righteous' worldly horizons of the Dean's flock and the limitless 'bliss' of divine food together in one assimilative event.

Dinesen is far too subtle a conteuse to insist we read *Babette's Feast* merely as a literal critique of certain kinds of religious faith. It is not simply that the outward trappings of faith are contrasted with a more authentic, inner experience of the sacred; but rather that Dinesen's concerns extend far beyond any specific doctrine or confession, gesturing towards transcendence and the way in which the community's rather sterile belief in the literal words and abstemious practices of the dead Dean comes to be transformed into a sacramental capacity to appreciate a God who exists in and through the world and His creatures rather than one who merely exists beyond it. When we eat food or relate to the other in the right spirit, Dinesen seems to be saying, we are touched by, we keep faith with, we are nourished by a sense of the other's inner presence. The other is 'food' within us: not swallowed whole in a fixed or frozen way, as with Dean's flock who have adhered slavishly to his precepts, but rather, as Kristeva suggests, absorbed metaphorically: digested in a creative, generative sense that continually multiplies, prolongs and deepens the profound and vivifying impact of its unseen presence in our lives. The logic of transubstantiation thus provides the conditions both for mourning and for psychic renewal; it is the means by which we symbolically replenish ourselves. 'Behold what you are!', exclaims St Augustine in his 57th sermon on the Eucharist, 'become what you receive!'. In receiving well, when we 'eat and drink in the right spirit' of Dinesen's Eucharistic hospitality perhaps, we open ourselves up to the advent of this incarnate, divine Other within; we assent to, we participate in, we become and are transformed by that which we have been given.

The psychoanalytic encounter

What does Dinesen's tale have to offer us as clinicians? It could certainly be argued that there are important differences between the dispensation of a sacrament and receiving psychotherapy. The former requires the presence of a priest and the operation of divine grace; and while there are those, like Foucault, and indeed Kristeva herself, who have aligned the position of the psychotherapist with that of a priest, the latter differs from a sacrament not least in terms of the extent to which its benefits might be perceived to be universally available. The story of Babette clearly draws on the Augustinian notion of a salvation that comes about simply through the grace of God, grace that is neither warranted nor earned. 'Grace', claims General Loewenhielm, 'makes no conditions and singles out none of us in particular' (p. 60); like Babette's lottery win, it is a gift that arrives when one is least expecting it. This freely given love cannot be willed, summoned or demanded, but can only be 'awaited with confidence and acknowledged in gratitude' (p. 60). By contrast, in a psychoanalysis we are dealing with the infinitely various and often intractable difficulties patients have in being able to receive what the analyst has to offer, vicissitudes which arguably limit the scope of therapeutic change and the possibilities for transformation.

If we turn to the role of the analyst, however, there seems to be a close affinity between what Dinesen sees as the condition of the soul required for the fruitful reception of the divine and the ethical position of the analyst who is asked to receive the patient's otherness. Perhaps we might think of Dinesen as someone who bids us do psychotherapy 'in the right spirit' by maintaining a radical receptiveness to the other in our clinical work, a receptiveness that I think has much in common with a Levinasian perspective where the patient as radical Other has an ethical claim on us. Levinas' emphasis on the face-to-face encounter with the other who bears the trace of God's face lays the ground for a psychotherapeutic encounter in which '[t]he Other remains infinitely transcendent, infinitely foreign' (1969, p. 194). Like Babette, whose 'foreign' presence interrupts and awakens the community in Berlevaag, the presence of otherness in the patient interrupts and awakens the therapist's subjectivity. Indeed, Dueck and Parsons (2007) point out that 'the self of the therapist is traumatized – fissured – by the otherness of the client' (p. 279). Just as metaphor inflates systems of signification to breaking point, so too there is a surplus of signification in the other that surpasses our capacity to absorb and contain its infinitude. Like Babette 'who had swelled and grown to such dimensions' (p. 45) that the anxious sisters see her forthcoming French dinner as 'a thing of incalculable nature and range' (p. 45), so the Other in Levinas is ontologically amplified, unassimilable, always already more than we can know or comprehend. Our ethical responsibility then is to regard the Other, as Dinesen's General does, as a 'not a moral, but a mystic, concern' (p. 52) and to bear the burden of his or her existence to the point of what Levinas calls 'substitution' or putting oneself in his or her place.

As a psychoanalyst, Kristeva is perhaps more attuned than is Levinas to the unsettling effects of the 'foreigner' within that act to constrain and delimit the kind of ethical encounter, the generosity and patience that Levinas proposes. Managing the sheer 'otherness' of one's inner unconscious and disruptive forces is necessary before entering into speech and relationships that can take account of 'otherness' in other people. But the ethic of waiting, service and sacrifice that Babette embodies and Levinas articulates is surely important in preparing the way for the advent of grace, a word that is scarcely mentioned in the psychotherapeutic literature at all. This is understandable, if only because the word is so heavily freighted with theological and doctrinal significance. But perhaps the idea of grace as a divine gift helps to disrupt and break the narcissistic, independent, 'bounded masterful self' (Cushman, 1990, p. 608) of Enlightenment rationality in which an investment of personal effort, agency and action is privileged over passivity, patience and sacrifice. Safran (2016), one of the very few psychoanalytic writers to address this topic, suggests that: 'Taken out of its theological context, the experience of grace simply entails the genuine recognition that there is a benevolent other who exists outside the realm of our subjective omnipotence, and the emergence of a receptivity to the emotional nurturance that this other can provide' (p. 70). Perhaps Ghent's (1999) notion of 'surrender', too, is closely aligned to the kind of receptivity that I think Dinesen gestures towards: a receptiveness which implies that 'however deeply buried or frozen, [there is] a longing for something in the environment to make possible the surrender, in the sense of yielding, of false self' (p. 214).

Paving the way in our clinical work for the reception of grace perhaps means to wait and serve the patient in the way he or she needs us to, just as Babette patiently agrees to serve split cod and ale-and-bread soup to the sisters. It also implies a willingness to be used in the service of a therapeutic process, a process in which 'neither the patient nor the analyst can bring about change through an act of will' (Safran, 2016, p. 63). These are ideas, of course, that will sit uneasily alongside much contemporary psychotherapeutic literature emphasising the need for evidence-based practice, effective outcomes and the evaluation of particular competences and skills in the therapist; and admittedly, the implications of *Babette's Feast* for clinical practice remain blurred and incomplete. But like all good parables, Dinesen's tale gives us no simple foothold in terms of praxis; instead, it provides only a bare outline which is intended to act as a spur to personal meaning and a stimulus to spiritual – and perhaps clinical – growth.

Conclusion

As I try to draw the threads of this chapter together, I realise I am now straining to contain the flood of ideas, images and theoretical concepts surging up within me in response to Dinesen's story. Notions of sacrifice, substitution, hospitality and gift, for example, remain particularly rich philosophical and psychotherapeutic seams yet to be quarried. But it is clear from the numerous writers and theorists who continue to find fresh insights and readings of Dinesen's text that the tale of Babette inevitably evokes a surplus of signification; an excess that perhaps indexes the very fecundity that is at the heart of the metaphoric process constitutive of her Eucharistic aesthetic. Rowan Williams (2003) writes: 'Every good story is about flesh becoming inhabited [...] life's uninhabited places breed a hunger for Spirit'; and there is certainly something in Dinesen's 'good story' that profoundly resonates with the mysteries I puzzled over so long ago as a seven-year-old preparing for my First Holy Communion. For Dinesen's parable invites us to consider the significance of the other's presence within us and to understand it not as a body to be devoured whole in fantasy, nor something merely to be captured by a static likeness, an image, a set of principles, doctrines or tenets, as the Dean's flock imagine. The arrival of the Stranger within, like the refugee Babette, rather has a metaphorical quality of transitivity, of continual 'carrying over', of savouring, perhaps, rather than swallowing. She embodies a direction rather than a destination. That we are called to remain receptive to the presence of this sacred Stranger, to remain faithful to the divine Other who is always in the process of coming is surely '[t]he true reason for Babette's presence in the two sisters' house' (p24).

I have suggested that the metaphorical process that Dinesen illuminates in her Eucharistic aesthetic is one that resonates deeply with the psychoanalytic project. From a wider perspective, however, her sacramental sensibility may be taken as constitutive of artistic creativity generally and of writing in particular. It is the artist whose sacramental imagination imbues the world with new significance and meaning, allowing us to see the universal in the particular, the everlasting in time, the transcendent in the immanent. It is the artist, like Dinesen herself, who is permeable or receptive to 'other' ways of seeing and experiencing, to new possibilities for creative living; it is she who provides us with what Kearney (2013) calls 'privileged portals to the hidden truths of the real' (p. 428). Indeed, in her radiant tale of Babette, Isak Dinesen offers up a rich feast of thought-provoking insights into some of the 'hidden truths' of both faith and psychoanalysis, gracing us all with her imagination, inspiration and artistry.

Notes

1 All references in the text to *Babette's Feast* are taken from Dinesen, I. (2013). *Babette's Feast and Other Stories*. London: Penguin Modern Classics.
2 The use of the term 'other' within psychoanalysis and philosophy refers to multiple, competing theoretical frameworks. Lacan, for example, distinguishes between the terms 'other' and 'Other', where the former designates the alienating status of the imaginary ego and the various ways in which misrecognition of the other as 'like' oneself serves to reduce its alterity. The big 'Other' by contrast refers to the symbolic order of law and language from which the subject derives meaning. Alterity, for Lacan, is thus conceptualised as subordinate to a signifying, linguistic system in which the paternal order establishes the position of subject and object. By contrast, writers such as Kristeva and Levinas regard the 'other' as unassimilable to the linguistic order of the sign, albeit in different ways and with widely differing consequences. Kristeva points to the identificatory processes by which the 'self' becomes 'other', pointing to the maternal alterity which underpins and disrupts the paternal order of law and language For Levinas, however, the radical, transcendent Other can be reduced neither to identification with the self nor to the systems of signification endorsed by Lacan. Detailed discussion of the different uses of the term 'other' lie beyond the scope of this chapter; for clarity, my use of the term 'other' should be taken to reference these latter frameworks in which the radical excess of the other is foregrounded as constitutive of subjectivity.

References

Abraham, N. and Torok, M. (1994). Mourning or melancholia: introjection versus incorporation. In: N.T. Rand (ed.), *The Shell and the Kernel: Renewals of Psychoanalysis*. Chicago and London: Chicago University Press.
Beck, E. (1998). Dinesen's Babette's Feast. *The Explicator*, 56, 4: 2010–2013.
Braune, K. (2007). *The Epistle of Paul to the Ephesians: An Exegetical and Doctrinal Commentary*, trans. M.B. Riddel. Eugene, OR: Wipf and Stock, 1871.

Clark, S. and Hulley, K. (1990). An interview with Julia Kristeva: cultural strangeness and the subject in crisis. *Discourses Journal for Theoretical Studies in Media and Culture*, 13, 1: 164–177.
Cushman, P. (1990). Why the self is empty. Towards a historically situated psychology. *American Psychologist*, 45, 5: 599–611.
Dinesen, I. (2013). *Babette's Feast and Other Stories*. London: Penguin Modern Classics.
Dueck, A. and Parsons, T. (2007). Ethics, alterity and psychotherapy: a Levinasian perspective. *Pastoral Psychology*, 55: 271–282.
Freud, S. (1917). Mourning and melancholia. In: J. Strachey (ed. and trans.), *The Standard Edition of the Complete Psychological Works of Sigmund Freud*, Vol. 14, pp. 237–258. London: Hogarth.
Freud, S. (1921). Group psychology and the analysis of the ego. In: J. Strachey (ed. and trans.), *The Standard Edition of the Complete Psychological Works of Sigmund Freud*, Vol. 18, pp. 65–144. London: Hogarth.
Freud, S. (1923). The Ego and the Id. In: J. Strachey (ed. and trans.), *The Standard Edition of the Complete Psychological Works of Sigmund Freud*, Vol. 19, pp. 1–66. London: Hogarth.
Kearney, R. (2010). Sacramental imagination: Eucharists of the ordinary universe in the works of Joyce, Proust and Woolf. In: H. Nelson, L. Szabo and J. Zimmermann (eds), *Through a Glass Darkly. Suffering, The Sacred and The Sublime in Literature and Theory*, pp. 183–222. Canada: Wilfred Laurier University Press. Kearney, R. (2013). Eucharistic imagination in Merleau-Ponty and James Joyce. In: F. O'Rourke (ed.), *Hidden Destinies: Philosophical Essays in Memory of Gerald Hanratty*. Notre Dame, IN: University of Notre Dame Press.
Kristeva, J. (1990). Identification and the real. In: P. Collier and H. Geyer-Ryan (eds), *Literary Theory Today*. Ithaca, NY: Cornell University Press.
Lane, P. (1999). An hour of millennium. A representation of the communion ritual in Babette's Feast. *The Oswald Review: An International Journal of Undergraduate Research and Criticism in the Discipline of English*, 1, 1: 21–26.
Levinas, E. (1969). *Totality and Infinity: An Essay on Exteriority*, trans. A. Lingis. Pittsburgh, NJ: Duquesne.
Mullins, M. (2009). Deeper down in the domain of human hearts: hope in Isak Dinesen's Babette's Feast. *Logos: A Journal of Catholic Thought and Culture*, 12, 1: 16–37.
O'Grady, K. (1997). The pun or the Eucharist? Eco and Kristeva on the consummate model for the metaphoric process. *Literature and Theology*, 11, 1: 93–115.
O'Rourke, M. (2012). *The Long Goodbye*. Hull: Riverhead Books.
Oliver, M. (2006). The vast ocean begins just outside our church: the Eucharist. In: *Thirst*, p. 24. Boston, MA: Beacon Press.
Rashkin, E. (2008). Devouring loss: a recipe for mourning in Babette's Feast. In: *Unspeakable Secrets and the Psychoanalysis of Culture*, pp. 25–46. New York: SUNY Press.
Ricoeur, P. (1975). Biblical hermeneutics. *Semeia*, 4: 89.
Robbe-Grillet, A. (1965). Nature, humanism and tragedy. In: *Snapshots and Towards a New Novel*, trans. B. Wright, p. 78. London: Calder and Boyars, 1958.
Safran, J. (2016). Agency, surrender, and grace in psychoanalysis. *Psychoanalytic Psychology*, 33, 1: 58–72.
Williams, R. (2003). From a lecture given at Sowerby Parish Church, Thirsk, February 2003. The First Bingen Lecture, Centre for Theology and Healing.
Wright, W. (1997). Babette's Feast: a religious film. *Journal of Religion and Film*, 1, 2: 1–28.

Chapter 6

'Familiar artifice'
Alice Munro's *The Moons of Jupiter*

> Men can do nothing without the make-believe of a beginning.
> George Eliot (1876)

Introduction

'Even as I most feverishly, desperately practise it', Alice Munro (1972) writes, 'I am a little afraid that the work with words may turn out to be a questionable trick, an evasion (and never more so than when it is most dazzling, apt and striking) an unavoidable lie' (p. 182). Munro's moral concern with artifice, with the way 'work with words' risks turning out to be a 'questionable trick', is something to which we might well pay heed. For these days, of course, everyone has a story. In popular culture there has been an exponential rise in the use of digital and social media along with self-help groups and other platforms enabling us to assemble, construct, narrate and defend our particular story: to fashion an identity through which we want to be known. As psychoanalysts, though, we might prefer, like Munro, to remain sceptical of the patient's – and indeed our own – 'work with words'; for the account of a life that is brought to therapy can all too readily be moulded into a sequential narrative akin to a novel, whose coherence is incommensurate with the fragmentary, irreconcilable or enigmatic aspects of experience. Well-rehearsed scripts and chronological plotlines establishing a seamless, self-directed, totalising account of the self's past, present and future not only alert us to the likely false connections woven into this smoothly narrated version of the self; they also signal the potential for an untrustworthy gap to open up between language at its 'most dazzling, apt and striking' and the complexity and intensity of the world it aims to describe.

The idea that the telling of the patient's story in therapy might be akin to the unfolding of a novel is not, of course, new. But we should ask what features of this literary genre might make it a suitable model for the telling of a self. There is a vast literature on the theory of the novel (see, e.g., Bakhtin, 1981; Lukacs, 1916; Mazzoni, 2017; McKeon, 2000) and considerable disagreement among literary theorists about how best to define the genre.

Indeed, the novel's long historical evolution and protean form make any attempt at specifying its distinguishing features almost impossible. However, Brooks (1984) reminds us how it has been 'the great nineteenth century narrative tradition' that 'conceived certain kinds of knowledge and truth to be inherently narrative, understandable (and expoundable) only by way of sequence, in a temporal unfolding' (p. xii). This interest in time and sequence, tied to the novel's 'central conventions of realism' (May, 2012, p. 176), is one that has most clearly come to influence the fields of counselling and psychotherapy. It lies embedded within notions of 'narrative coherence' (Schafer, 1980) and 'autobiographical competence' (Holmes, 1993) and in the attempt to produce a narrative 'I' that can tell its own story: an active quest for reality and identity that is deemed by some (e.g. Roberts, 2000) to be the principal aim and function of therapy. Yet if the purpose of psychoanalysis is, as Steedman (1992) suggests, 'to give back to the patient the story of his or her life, welded into a chronological sequence and narrative coherence, so that at the end of it all, the coming to psychic health might be seen as the re-appropriation of one's own life story' (p. 172), then we might want to ask, as does Walsh (2017), whether and to what extent the psychoanalytic subject is able to give any account of him- or herself that does not recruit the linear, sequential mode of narrative typical of the novel.

By way of interrogating these novelistic forms of discourse in some currently popular models of therapy, I want to propose a possible alternative literary form that Freud himself suggests in his early case histories. Freud was notoriously dismayed by the way these appeared to read more like short stories than scientific treatises (Freud and Breuer, 1895). 'I must console myself', he writes in his case history of Elisabeth von R., 'with the reflection that the nature of the subject is evidently responsible for this, rather than any preference of my own' (p. 160). Freud's own 'work with words' here is already mobilising the 'questionable trick' of which Munro speaks; for the idea of something 'in the nature of the subject' leaves us wondering whether Freud is referring to the subject in terms of the field, the discipline of psychoanalysis, or whether he is hinting at the psychoanalytic subject in terms of the self and its constitution. I take seriously the latter idea: that there is something in the nature of the self and how it is brought into being that might require something closer to the form of a short story for its articulation than the narrative modes of telling so often favoured within contemporary therapeutic culture.

Why might this be so? The relationship between psychoanalysis and literature has traditionally been seen by some (e.g. Derrida, 1975; Felman, 1977; Kirova, 1997) as a troubled one, as I have briefly discussed in the introduction and elsewhere (Rizq, 2018). Moving on from these arguments, however, I want to start by thinking of narrative as a way of presenting reality to the mind: of stories as a kind of epistemological category (Jameson 1989). Of interest here are the literary methods of the short story, and the means by which the reader is oriented to a particular kind of experience and knowledge of the world and the self. It is beyond my scope here to detail in full the range and variety of ways this is said to be different from the kind of knowledge and experience that is conveyed by the novel. But we might remember that the realist novel, especially the *Bildungsroman,* aims to generate an illusion of life by revealing actions and everyday details of the social, psychological and material world that confer a sense of authenticity and verisimilitude. It aims to offer a coherent, well-plotted narrative with an emphasis on resolution of conflict. Modernist novels have, of course, significantly complicated these features, aiming to 'illumine the mind within' as Virginia Woolf (1929) argues, 'rather than the world without' (p. 121) by creating an illusion of (mental) life via an intense focus on the minute details of a shifting inner consciousness and the vagaries of personal subjectivity. And while postmodernism has since considerably problematised and extended its formal possibilities, the novel's overriding concern with fullness, plenitude and an extensive view of the world – including the inner world – could be said to contrast with the short story's focus on the momentary, the singular and the revelatory.

The short story can be understood as a form that is 'compressed, unified and plotted' (Patea, 2012, p. 3), rendering perception 'in a mode close to the way in which we experience and know the world: occasionally, in fragments' (p. 19). By virtue of its brevity and concision, it is capable of generating for the reader a kind of experience quite different from that engendered by the novel. It rests on something closer to a metaphysical ontology, created by a focus not on the temporality and linearity of everyday life but rather on what Baxter (2008) calls the 'widened moment' that refuses to recast 'the incommensurate into an arbitrary continuity' (Trussler, 1996, p. 562). The novel, particularly the 'standard novel of plotted suspense' (Rader, 1993, p. 80, note 6), commonly recruits an explanatory epistemology and proceeds by way of specifying the contextual details that render the social world recognisable and familiar. The short story, by contrast, tends to recruit a revelatory epistemology, proceeding via a 'logic of unveiling' (Baxter, 2008) that generates a moment of secular epiphany or insight. Novels are frequently discursive, aiming to expand or embroider on a particular theme, while a short story is capable of condensing or distilling experience. It is likely to focus on a single event, emotion or situation, aiming to capture the essence of a feeling or experience. It conveys, as Poe (1842) suggests, a 'unity of impression' or a single, self-contained effect. Finally, from an historical perspective, the novel stems from the oral tradition of the saga and the epic: lengthy, complex forms rooted in the classical stories of travel, warfare and heroic deeds. The short story, by contrast, is a briefer narrative form deriving from the ancient traditions of myth, biblical verse, parable, fable and romance. It is bound up with the experience of the sacred. Indeed, in its tendency to engage with what Rohrberger (2004) calls 'a mystical world of paradox and ambiguity, of shadows and shifting perspectives governed not by rational order but by intuition and dream logic' (p. 6), we might say that the short story constitutes 'not a form of knowledge, but a challenge to knowledge' (Leitch, 1989, p. 133).

While there is a growing academic literature on the short story (e.g. Lounsberry et al., 1998; May, 1996, 2013; O'Connor, 1963; Rohrberger, 2004), I do not intend, and nor is it within my area of expertise, to elaborate on the theory of the genre. Rather, I want to borrow from literary criticism to focus more narrowly on what it is about the short story's particular 'way of telling' that might shed light on the account of a life that occurs within a psychoanalysis. In this chapter, I will use the example of Munro's (1983) *The Moons of Jupiter,* a collection of short stories in which she offers a sequence of eleven tales plotting the lives and experiences of women at different stages of their lives. The content of each story varies enormously, but all revolve round her protagonists' shared experiences of work, relationships and family life as well as their confrontation with ageing and death. The final title story of the collection is justly celebrated not only by Munro's reading public but also by a number of literary critics including Howells (1998), who suggests that *The Moons of Jupiter* 'is arguably the most significant turning point in Munro's fiction-writing career' (p. 67). Mayberry (2009) calls it 'one of Munro's most intensely focused examinations of the capabilities and limitations of narrative' (p. 30). While these and a number of other critics, notably Carrington (1989), Heble (1994), McIntyre (2009) and Redekop (1992) provide stimulating close readings of the story, none of them sets out specifically to examine the implications for a psychoanalytic understanding of the self and its constitution. I am aware, of course, this territory includes debates and theoretical ideas that are likely to be extremely familiar to psychoanalysts and literary critics alike; but I hope to approach the topic as freshly as possible via an exploration of the kind of subjectivity Munro describes and dramatises in her particular way of telling in the story. Indeed, the purpose of this chapter is not to offer a psychoanalytic reading of Munro's tale, thereby perpetuating the privileged theoretical position often assumed by psychoanalysis over literature - what Felman (1977, p. 5) has called a 'relationship of subordination' - so much as to find new ways of illuminating psychoanalytic ideas through my reading of her short story. Accordingly, I will remain close to Munro's own logic which consistently focuses on the limits inherent in language and representation. Lacanian metapsychology, with its problematic of the real, offers an important touchstone here, as does Keenan's (1997) philosophy of reading, which interrogates the fable in order to explore how subjectivity is installed in the reader via a process of substitution and identification. I will go on to offer a re-reading of Freud's (1913) *Totem and Taboo,* where I follow Lacan in taking the view that the self finds itself in the image of the other. I suggest that, like *The Moons of Jupiter, Totem and Taboo* may be seen as an exemplary tale laying bare the fictive origins of the self. I will conclude that the short story's fabular lineage makes it a particularly suitable literary model for the constitution of the self within psychoanalysis.

The Moons of Jupiter[1]

In the opening pages of *The Moons of Jupiter*, we find a middle-aged divorced Janet settling her elderly father into the heart wing of a Toronto hospital. He is wired up to an ECG: 'On the screen', says Janet,

> a bright jagged line was continually being written. The writing was accompanied by nervous electronic beeping. The behaviour of his heart was on display. I tried to ignore it. It seemed to me that paying such close attention – in fact, dramatizing what ought to be a most secret activity – was asking for trouble.
>
> (pp. 217–8)

The alert reader will be aware, even at this early point in Munro's tale, that the 'jagged line' that is 'continually being written' here is not simply an erratic heartbeat. It points a metafictional finger, so to speak, at the act of writing itself: the art of representing the heart's 'most secret activity', something that is usually taken to be invisible. But what is it about 'paying such close attention' to writing that leads to trouble? Munro's carefully-choreographed and extraordinarily stylised story of only a few pages illuminates how the artifice of language inevitably distances us from reality; and how narrative design and order as well as the act of naming in the story rely on the mimetic power of language to evoke mystery, pathos and an elegiac sense of loss in the reader while at the same time performing its ineluctable failure to adequately represent the world, the self and the other.

Janet is coming to terms with the impending death of her father as well the refusal of her eldest adult daughter to communicate with her. The story, told over seven short sections that loop back and forth over the space of a few days is not only of how she makes the complex inner psychological adjustments necessary to confront the task of mourning and letting go within her family relationships; it is a tale that dramatises how Janet achieves moments of a new self-awareness. It seems unlikely then that Munro's decision to arrange her material in seven, non-sequential sections is arbitrary; for like the biblical time-span of seven days that God takes to create the world, Janet herself has limited time before her father's operation to create a new emotional world. She will do so by restoring a lost sense of connection and understanding with him as well as with her eldest daughter. The story's lack of narrative linearity - Janet's four hospital visits, an overnight stay at her youngest daughter's flat, the visit to the planetarium and a tranquil moment of rest in a Chinese garden - vividly conveys the way Janet's consciousness and memory orbit around her family and loved ones. A muddled chronology, defying easy summary, not only mirrors the muddle and disorder of life; it mimes the way in which Janet's memory works retroactively to rework and revise her understanding of her relationships as well as of herself.

Janet herself is a writer and the reader is given to understand that she will struggle with the versions of other people she has created in her mind. We see how this makes it difficult for Janet to face and cope with her father's manifest vulnerability and to think about him as a person with an independent life and history of his own. She knows that, as a young boy, he ran away from home in search of a better life, but she hadn't cared 'to think of his younger selves' she admits. 'Even his bare torso, thick and white … was a danger to me; it looked so strong and young. The wrinkled neck, the age-freckled hands and arms, the narrow, courteous head, with its thin gray hair and mustache, were more what I was used to' (p. 220). It is clear then that Janet's relationship with her father is predicated on a story she has fabricated around him: 'his independence, his self-sufficiency, his forbearance' (p. 220). When she tells people about him, she insists: 'He worked in a factory, he worked in his garden, he read history books […] he never made a fuss' (p. 220).

But following the news that her eldest daughter, Nichola, wants to be 'incommunicado for a while' (p. 221), Janet begins to examine herself afresh. Wryly recalling her younger self with her own friends, she thinks, 'How thoroughly we dealt with our fathers and mothers, deplored their marriages, their mistaken ambitions or fear of ambition, how competently we filed them away, defined them beyond any possibility of change. What presumption' (p. 222). Indeed, Janet now starts to realise that what she believes about Nichola – that she is 'sly and solitary, cold, seductive' (p. 223) – is likely to be contradicted by others who know otherwise. On returning to the hospital, she begins to question her understanding of her father, recognising that the version she has always held of him is partial, coloured by her own perspective, and distorted by self-interest. It was not true that 'he never spoke regretfully about his life' she realises. 'It was just that I didn't listen' (p. 225).

But in the face of his imminent heart operation, her father too is reworking his own version of himself as part of his preparations for death. A further fiction is invoked as he quotes the line 'Shoreless seas', from 'Columbus', a poem by Joaquim Miller that he is trying to recall. Like the jagged lifeline of the ECG that illuminates the heart's vital, yet hidden biological rhythms, poetry here illuminates the heart's essential yet concealed psychological activity as it prepares for its final journey towards death and the New World of the unknown. Yet scepticism about the capacity of poetry or any fiction to console in the face of mortality remains foregrounded: 'If there's anything you can't explain right away, there's a great temptation to – well, to make a mystery out of it' (p. 226) he remarks; and Janet, 'feeling an appalling rush of love and recognition' (p. 226), believes her father is referring to the soul. But both maintain a certain wariness about the false comforts of religion that mean 'playing tricks on yourself' (p. 226). Inasmuch as Janet's father wants to believe in the stories he has been reading in magazines that tell of people's comforting near-death experiences, he maintains a level of suspicion, if not outright cynicism, when faced with any attempt to make death meaningful, comprehensible and bearable: 'It's all in whether you want to believe that kind of thing or not' (p. 226).

Janet's visit to the planetarium, ostensibly to distract herself from her anxiety about her father's impending operation, unmistakably signals the central event of the story. As she sits down with an audience of noisy schoolchildren, a theatrical presentation announced by 'some splendid, commanding music' (p. 230) turns the bowl of the planetarium's ceiling into dark blue night sky, 'an orchestrated image' according to Howells (1998) 'of infinite space inside a closed dome' (p. 83). It is at once a mythic vision of the cosmos, dramatising the shifting patterns of a universe whose distant meaning lies beyond any human understanding, as well as an image of the patterning of meaning that constitutes the narrative text. The immensity and significance of the transcendent vision is set alongside the apparent banality and meaninglessness of everyday life, indexed here by the audience of indifferent children 'crackling their potato-chip bags' (p. 230). At first it is the illusion of reality that is foregrounded – 'the stars came out not all at once but one after the other the way stars really do come out at night, though more quickly' (p. 230) – and the 'stunning facts' are confidently listed to convey the 'innumerable repetitions, innumerable variations' (p. 231) of the galaxies within the universe. Subsequently, though, we are told 'realism was abandoned, for familiar artifice' (p. 231); a model or map of the solar system is invoked to convey in more 'elegant style' the movement of the planets within the vast cosmos. Indeed we, like the audience watching the show, are being offered different ways of representing and dramatising the unfathomable, unknowable and mysterious workings of the universe and our place within it. A sense of the radical insufficiency of any knowledge obtained by these forms of representation is, however, always present. Janet learns that Mercury now rotates three times as it circles around the sun, instead of just once as was previously understood. These updated facts about planetary activity mirror on a cosmic scale the way in which Janet is in the process of updating the meaning and significance of events and relationships in her life. Knowledge can only ever be provisional: 'Why did they give out such confident information, only to announce later that it was quite wrong' (p. 231)? Janet's scepticism here is not only about the validity of scientific knowledge; it registers Munro's profound doubts about the capacity of language to model the world and to frame life's excess and complexity in all its 'innumerable repetitions, innumerable variations'. Perhaps it is not surprising then that at the end of the show, Janet remains unimpressed by the artifice behind the presentation: 'the music, the church-like solemnity, simulating the awe that they supposed they ought to feel' (pp. 231–2). The cosmic drama she has watched fails to do justice to the 'horrible immensities' (p. 231) of the universe; and like the children who do not comment on what they have seen but are more interested in 'eatables and further entertainment' (p. 231) she refuses the comforting vision of transcendence on offer much as her father has earlier refused the false comfort offered by the magazine stories of near-death experiences. Awe, she feels, is something to be felt only in the face of the real: 'once you knew what it was, you wouldn't be courting it' (p. 232).

Returning to the hospital for her father's last night before the operation, Janet says that she has been to an 'exciting' show at the planetarium, telling him 'it's like a slightly phony temple' (p. 232). She immediately regrets her comment: 'I had meant that to be truthful, but it sounded slick and superior' (p. 232). The limitations of words to convey truth can be shaming, Munro hints, not only because they utterly fail to convey the reality of experience and mortality, but because, like the word 'exciting', they can also convey something false: something closer to a caricature than the truth. Ashamed of her 'slick and superior' language, Janet makes a final effort to forge an emotional connection with her father as she asks him to list the moons of Jupiter, and they engage in the mutual attempt to remember and name each one: Io, Europa, Ganymede, Callisto. Naming here, for Munro, is much more than simply providing a label; for here, the process of naming the moons testifies to the power of fiction to create and shape the universe into a satisfying story. The Greek characters after whom the moons are named are rooted in mythology, a classical narrative used to understand and manage the mysteries of the universe. It is this mythical narrative that is recruited by Janet and her father to create an illusion of comfort before their inevitable parting.

The seventh and final section concludes the story with a flashback to Janet's brief sojourn in a Chinese garden after she left the planetarium the previous day. As Janet sits peacefully on her own, the re-arranged chronology in the story allows Munro to hint at the biblical day of rest following God's creation of the world. Like the story itself, the garden too is a fiction, a representation of something that belongs to another time and place; but its 'familiar artifice', like the planetarium's, seems to calm and soothe Janet before she returns to the hospital for the final meeting with her father. In the distance, she sees 'a girl who reminded [her] of Nichola' (p. 233) and realises that just as she will have to let her father go into his operation, so too she will have to let Nichola go into adult life, independent of her mother: 'She was one of the grown up people in the world now' (p. 233).

Forms of stories

'I don't really understand a novel', says Munro (quoted in Rothstein, 1986).

> I don't understand where the excitement is supposed to come in a novel, and I do in a story. There's a kind of tension that if I'm getting a story right I can feel right away, and I don't feel that when I try to write a novel. I kind of want a moment that's explosive, and I want everything gathered into that.
>
> (p. 17)

If, as May (1984) argues, 'the short story is short precisely because of the kind of experience or reality embodied in it' (p. 328), then perhaps it is by way of the 'explosive' moment that we can best grasp the genre's most fundamental way of telling. For unlike the novel that is propelled by its relationship to what E. M. Forster (1927) calls 'the naked worm of time', a narrative of events or experiences generally arranged in linear sequence, the short story is driven by its relationship to the epiphanic moment: a moment that, by virtue of being extracted from the flow of time, comes to be imbued with particular significance and power. Indeed, as a literary mode that remains close to fable and folklore, as May (1984) reminds us, the short story is acutely sensitive to the manifestation of what Cassirer (1946) refers to as the 'momentary deity': a primitive mode of experience constituted by a 'fleeting, emerging and vanishing mental content' piercing everyday life with an experience of the uncanny or sacred. 'In stark uniqueness and singleness it confronts us', writes Cassirer,

> not as part of some force which may manifest itself here, there and everywhere, in various places and times, and for different persons, but as something that exists only here and now, in one indivisible moment of experience, and for only one subject whom it overwhelms and holds in thrall.
>
> (p. 18)

Gordimer (1976) describes the short story's attempt to depict this ephemeral, phenomenological quality of experience as akin to seeing by 'the flash of fireflies, in and out, now here, now there, in darkness' (p. 264). It is a metaphor that vividly evokes the simultaneous, transient glimpses of the universe that Munro describes in the planetarium scene: 'the way the stars came out not all at once but one after the other the way stars really do come out at night, though more quickly'. Munro captures this momentary, dissolving perception of that which lies beneath life's surface appearances by embedding it not within a chronologically-arranged sequence of episodes over time, but within a more paratactic arrangement: a loose cohesion of incidents that prohibits any easy recourse to presumed connections, reasons or motives. The story's seven separate sections index various events taking place over a few days in Janet's life. Juxtaposed rather than explicitly connected, they are related in a way that is never unambiguously thematised allowing Munro to simply point to events rather than attempting to explain their relationship to each other. Indeed, the idea that we might be able to establish a causal connection between contingent events, that we might be able to mould the direction of our lives into a comforting explanatory narrative, is precisely the kind of self-deceiving fiction that Munro's story seeks both to dramatise and unsettle.

The elimination of causal connections alongside the story's tightly-knit unity of form ensures the reader has to work hard to establish the possible interrelationships between disparate elements in the tale as well as to grasp what is hinted at or obscured beneath the surface of the text. It is not until the planetarium scene that the reader is presented with what we might think of as the central *mise en abyme*: a scaled-down mirror version of the wider universe that is also a version of Munro's fictive world. It confronts the reader with an explosively dense metafictional moment in which Munro finally lays bare the artifice that underlies our experience of the world and its 'horrible immensities'. It gestures towards the radical insufficiency of language even while it exploits it as a medium that comforts us with 'stunning facts' or traditional narratives seeking to reassure and explain. The patterns of the stars, the constellations that Janet sees in the bowl of the planetarium, the scientific models by which we understand the universe are only human constructions imposed on a vast, enigmatic, ineffable universe. 'Constellations do not exist', writes Milner (2016), 'there only exist the stars that compose them' (p. 31). Like Janet, we look up at the starry sky and persuade ourselves that we can see meaningful patterns emerging from the formless cosmic flux above. The Great Bear and Little Bear that Janet subsequently mentions to her father in the hospital are created entirely within the imagination; yet somehow they appear to us still, radiantly shining out from the night sky. We navigate the external universe by weaving the chaos of the stars into meaningful patterns, forms and names in the same way as we navigate the internal subjective world by constructing patterns of meaning out of the fragments of our experience, from the disparate events and contingencies of our lives. Indeed, when Janet and her father work together in their final meeting to name the moons of Jupiter, their joint effort brings, quite literally, the 'momentary deity' into existence. The names of Io, Europa, Ganymede, Callisto of course derive from classical mythology, itself a series of fictional narratives intended to render the vast intricacies of the universe explicable to the ancients Greeks. Munro seems here to be calling on the short story's earliest traditions to underline the way naming, giving words to things, itself constructs how we perceive, pattern and understand the world. Yet it is in her very attempt to narrate experience, to 'dramatize what ought to be a most secret activity' that Munro performs the 'questionable trick' of writing. By drawing attention to her story as a work of art, as well as to the role of the writer in fashioning or fictioning the world, Munro aims to interrogate, disrupt and unsettle our ideas about our relationship to reality.

The short story as fable

Perhaps these notions of fashioning and fictioning bring us closer to the roots of the short story in fable. The etymology of the word *fable* derives from the Latin *fari*, to speak, as well as the Greek *pharein* to say. From *fari* we derive fate, that which is spoken, and *fabula*, an account or story, something that is fabricated. To speak, it seems, is always to tell a tale; yet as Voltaire (1747) comments in the dedicatory letter to *Zadig*, a fable is an 'ouvrage qui dit plus qu'il ne semble dire' (p. 22) – a work which says more than it seems to say. Indeed, in the past, fables were often taken to be mythologies, animistic folktales requiring interpretation to uncover what Smith (1915) calls 'some general truth pertinent solely to man' (p. 524). While not all short stories are fables, it is certainly true that fables themselves are generally brief, sometimes extremely so; and so we might say, in Gelley's (1995) words, that the fable is a short tale that aims to articulate 'narrative examples and moral meanings' (p. 122). It provides a model of ethical conduct not via moral instruction or didactic teaching but rather via instances or comparisons. Something is brought to the reader's awareness by way of a likeness, an Aristotelian illustration or *paradeigma* inductively pointing to further examples of a more general theme or category. Examples function, suggests Aristotle, 'by moving from particular to particular, passing through the universal' offering 'a particular and practical conclusion that is an indication for concrete acting' (quoted in Natali, 1989, p. 147). If we stand back for a moment to position *The Moons of Jupiter* within the context of the ten other stories making up Munro's collection, we can see that the entire book revolves around a series of iterative examples comprising the 'innumerable repetitions' and 'innumerable variations' of women's lives.

However, Ambuel (2007) reminds us that we need to account for a certain philosophical ambiguity in the notion of a *paradeigma;* for the term refers both to a particular instance or example as well as to the transcendental ideal on which all other instances or examples model themselves. 'A *paradeigma* might be an architect's or sculptor's model, an image (*eikōn*) of what is to be made' he writes, 'but it can also be an exemplar, the standard against which other things are measured' (p. 8). But what might this mean in Munro's tale? For it is not as if she is asking us to accept *The Moons of Jupiter* as an example of how to behave; or that Janet is being held up as a kind of moral ideal for us to emulate. Rather, hidden within her story lies the deeper question about language and its relationship to the reality we inhabit. To what extent, and with what effect, Munro asks, can the fiction that is language stand as an example of the world it describes and illuminates? Can it say anything truthful, or does its deployment of 'dazzling, apt and striking' words merely mislead us? Munro's scepticism comes to the fore in the central exemplum of the planetarium where, by juxtaposing Janet's world of relationships alongside the sidereal world of the cosmos, she foregrounds the imaginative partnership inevitably entailed by our contact with the world. Like Janet, we too are confronted by 'familiar artifice', the fictions by which we understand the 'horrible immensities' of the universe. But are these 'ordinary "illusions"' (Seligman, 2018, p. 267) merely a kind of ornamental 'cover' used to stretch over the reality of the world, like the ceiling of the planetarium? Or is there something about the world itself that demands this covering, this fiction, in order to display itself at all? Pushing at these questions a little further, we can see it is not that fiction offers us a limited version of reality, a replica that convincingly simulates the world while unfortunately lacking authenticity in this or that respect; or that it enables us to find ways of modelling things that already exist in the world. The metaphysical opposition between reality and fiction is not to be resolved by recourse to a fictional model purporting to represent the reality of the world. Instead, Munro seems to suggest, it is through the act of writing, of inventing a story, that we are able to fashion or fiction a world for ourselves; that we can bring the world itself into being. Yet even as Munro undertakes this creative act, she remains deeply mistrustful of its authority. She deploys 'artifice' as a means of fictioning a world whose claim to a relationship of verisimilitude remains continually open to doubt. Indeed, in ensuring 'realism [gives] way to familiar artifice', Munro fashions a world whose invented origins, as we shall see, embody and instate a truth about the fiction that inaugurates the self.

The short story as fable of the subject

Fables of course, are principally allegories: brief stories used as models of ethical action. 'The fable', writes Keenan (1997), 'is offered for example, but for the kind of example that asks to happen in an act of something like imitation or identification, in the rhetorical event of a comparison' (p. 46). What does this mean, and how might the notion of the fable as exemplary tale help us understand the relationship between the short story and the psychoanalytic concept of the subject? In his philosophical theory of reading, Keenan draws on the Aesopian fable of the raven that pretends to be an eagle to illuminate the way identification with the other forms the borrowed basis of the self. Starting off without a name of his own, the raven decides to call himself an eagle hoping to catch a lamb in his claws like a bird of prey. Captured by a shepherd after failing in his hubristic task, the raven is interrogated about what kind of bird he is. He responds by re-telling the fable and calling himself 'raven' for the first time, thus restoring to himself a name he never knew he had. 'The raven speaks', writes Keenan, 'and finally says, "I am", starting from a feint, a fiction, a borrowed figure' (p. 67). The reader of the fable, he suggests, is similarly asked to identify with the story's protagonist: to compare him- or herself with the raven and 'to assume its name and follow its example, in order to learn not to compare yourself with what you're not' (p. 66). Like the raven who has made the error of substituting himself for another, then, the reader is recruited by the fable's address into miming the very rhetorical mechanism of substitution by which the protagonist comes into being as a subject. It is an error, suggests Keenan, that consigns subjectivity to a constitutive alterity of which it will always remain unconscious.

Keenan's interest lies in the way reading restores subjectivity, installing a certain responsibility in the face of the undecidable. But it is what he has to say about the fabular basis of the self that I think most helps us freshly approach the issues of self-formation raised by Munro's story. I want to return to Freud here, for in the final essay of *Totem and Taboo* (1912–13), he was once again to write a short story: not a case history this time, but rather a story about the anthropological origins of the Oedipus complex and the foundation of society, religion and culture. In his tale, Freud proposes a decisive, historical event in primitive times: the existence of a tyrannical, primal Father and the tribal horde of sons who kill and devour him. This 'memorable and criminal deed', Freud suggests, marked the beginning of religious principles and moral restrictions as feelings of guilt and remorse in the band of brothers led eventually to the creation of taboos. In my re-reading of Freud, I am mindful of Lacan's (1959–60a) view that 'the important feature of *Totem and Taboo* is that it is a myth' (p. 176); indeed, as he writes elsewhere, 'the myth is more like a fable' (Note 7, p. 115). Like Aesop's fable of the raven and the eagle, then, I want to suggest *Totem and Taboo* can be read as a fiction that has something to tell us about the constitution of the self, about how we come to consciousness of ourselves as subjects through identification with the other.

While Strachey (1955) tells us that Freud regarded *Totem and Taboo* as his best written work, it is clear that Freud himself had considerable doubts about its publication. His anxiety can be inferred from a short footnote to the paper: 'The lack of precision in what I have written in the text above, its abbreviation of the time factor and its compression of the whole subject matter, may be attributed to the reserve necessitated by the nature of the topic' (p. 141). Perhaps it is worth pausing here; for Freud's choice of words, his reservation about 'the nature of the topic', is strangely reminiscent of the words used in his case history of Elisabeth von R. some 18 years earlier. We might recall that in that work, Freud expresses concern about how there is something 'in the nature of the subject' that means his case histories are likely to be read as short stories rather than scientific reports. In *Totem and Taboo*, Freud's worry resurfaces again in his references to the 'abbreviation of time' and 'compression of the whole subject matter', characteristics that, as we have seen, may be considered to be the sine qua non of the short story yet which Freud feels – with some dismay, perhaps – lend 'a monstrous air' (p. 141) to his hypothesis.

In his daring tale of sacrificial parricide, Freud suggests that the tribal brothers unite over their hatred of and ambivalence towards the authoritative Father of prehistory. 'The violent, primal father', he writes (1913), 'had doubtless been the feared and envied model of each one of the company of brothers; and in the act of devouring him they accomplished their identification with him, and each one of them acquired a portion of his strength' (p. 142). Killing the father, Freud seems to suggest here, takes place neither out of the sons' wish for revenge nor out of jealousy of his sexual privilege, but rather in order to acquire his power and identity for themselves. In this way, the eating of the primal Father, the totem meal that incorporates the other within the self, implies the annihilation of the other who is now the constitutive foundation of the self. 'I the ego am born by assimilating the other, by devouring him, incorporating him' writes Borch-Jacobsen (1993) in his provocative discussion of Freud's paper. 'Everything ... begins with murderous, blind identification, all the blinder because there is still no ego to see anything or represent anything to itself at all' (p. 33). Reading *Totem and Taboo* in this dark vein reverses the notion of identification Freud (1917) was subsequently to propose in *Mourning and Melancholia*, where identification is seen as a form of desire ('identification is a preliminary stage of object-choice' [p. 249]). Here, desire is instead understood as identification and we are given an example of the identity of an ego that cannot pre-exist the event of imitation, of identification; it is as if the very essence of subjectivity lies not within the self, but within the other who is desired as model. '[T]he imitant', says Lacoue-Labarthe (1990), 'has to be nothing in and of itself or must [...] have "nothing characteristic of itself". I must not therefore already be a subject' (p. 82). It seems then we can only come into being, we can only be created, through identification. It is a borrowing of that which will never be returned, a ruthless plagiarising of the other through which we incorporate an identity whose alterity we subsequently repress or eliminate. Through this act of identification the desiring subject, the one who longs to be a subject as the other is a subject, is inaugurated.

But what can it be 'in the nature of the topic' that makes Freud protest further on in his footnote that '[i]t would be as foolish to aim at exactitude in such questions as it would be unfair to insist on certainty' (p. 141)? Along with Lacan (1959–60b), who comments, ironically, that '[w]e have seen orangutans. But not the slightest trace has ever been seen of the father of the horde' (p. 113), I would like to suggest that whatever else it is, Freud's wonderfully speculative story is an exemplary tale; indeed, it is one that Freud (1921) himself was subsequently to call a 'Just-so Story' (p. 122). It mimes the inexactitude, the undecidability of its own fabulous origins. We might remember that Freud at first seems to argue that the putative historical accuracy of the events he describes is irrelevant: the reality might never have taken place at all. The sons' remorse could have been provoked as much by the phantasy of killing the father as by actually killing him in reality: 'the mere existence of a wishful *phantasy* of killing and devouring him', he writes, 'would have been enough to produce the moral reaction that created totemism and taboo ... psychical reality would be strong enough to bear the weight of these consequences' (p. 160). But Freud's concern about the 'lack of precision' in his hypothesis only serves to make him all the more determined to make a case for the decisive priority of the actual event's occurrence in reality. In making a comparison with modern day neurotics, he argues: '[N]eurotics are above all *inhibited* in their actions: for them, the thought is the complete substitute for the deed. Primitive men, on the other hand', he writes, 'are *uninhibited*: thought passes directly into action' (p. 161). For primitive men, then, the deed is pre-eminent. It takes priority over something which in the neurotic will remain at the level of psychic phantasy. And so it is the originary act, the primal murder, which appears to constitute the basis of Freud's triumphant conclusion: 'In the beginning was the Deed' (p. 161).

But in another apparently minor footnote, almost an *esprit de l'escalier* at the end of the paper, Freud enigmatically refers this final phrase back to a scene in Goethe's *Faust*. It is the moment in which Faust translates the first few lines of Genesis ('In the beginning was the Word') and, dissatisfied, finds himself substituting 'deed' for 'Word' in precisely the gesture that Freud himself has just plagiarised. In other words, Freud's claim to verisimilitude appears to lean not on the authenticity of a potentially verifiable historical event, but rather on a borrowed fictional text, on another Word. Like Faust, Freud is attempting to substitute an act for what is, in fact, a fiction. But if the primal murder, the Deed, is seen as merely a substitute for what will later become, in neurotics, the phantasy of killing the Father, we might say that the authority of Freud's tale rests on the undecidability of a prior fiction, on the generation of a (primal) fantasy now deemed to be the precondition for an invented beginning. Following Keenan then, it seems the eagle that is *Totem and Taboo* turns out to be a raven after all. It is an exemplary tale, a fable in which Freud stages the very act of identification, of substitution, that itself inaugurates his story of the founding Father, which is to say it is a fable about the origin of fable itself. By telling us a fictive story of origins folded within another founding tale, Freud (1913) lays bare 'the origin of so many things – of social organisation, of moral restrictions, and of religion' (p. 142), exposing them to the artifice of their beginnings.

We are beginning to approach more nearly here how the short story's fabular lineage makes it a genre particularly suited to dramatising the project of self-knowledge and its limits. Like most of Munro's characters, Janet is a writer and storyteller whose memory appears to be the principal source and repository of a growing self-awareness. But Munro alerts the reader to the way in which Janet's memory has formed the basis of a self whose origins lie in a necessary fiction: necessary not just because of some token admission of our limited capacity to know and understand the self, but because of Munro's awareness of the ineluctable limits to self-possession. When Janet reviews the narrative of her life, she becomes aware, as Cavarero (2000) points out, that '[a]utobiographical memory always recounts a story that is incomplete from the beginning. It is necessary to go back to the narration told by others, in order for the story to begin from where it really began' (p. 39). The stories the adult Janet tells about herself and her father have their roots in her earliest experiences at home in the family, with those who knew her best. Yet even here as she comes to realise, the status of her self-knowledge is precarious. She remembers the words of her father: 'You know those years you were growing up – well, that's all just a kind of a blur to me' (p. 222). In turn, she reflects on herself as a young parent who 'couldn't tell the years apart' (p. 223), and thinks regretfully about her exhaustion and forgetfulness at the time her daughters were born. It seems as if the first chapter in the story of a life is inescapably registered as a loss, even by those whom we have most trusted to keep, sustain and treasure it.

The quest for self-knowledge, for the self's story of itself, can therefore only ever begin with a fiction, 'a refabulation', says Cavarero (2000), 'of a story told by others' (p. 39). Indeed, we might recall that the poem by Joaquim Miller that Janet's father tries to remember is itself a refabulation. It is both a tale told by Columbus's shipmate about the discovery of America as well as the re-telling of a founding story of origins. Munro's insertion of Miller's poem stages this re-telling by offering us the story of a tale wrapped within a fable that is itself contained within a fiction. In *The Moons of Jupiter*, just as in *Totem and Taboo*, 'realism [gives] way to familiar artifice', offering the reader an exemplary tale about the death of the Father that founds a New World, with both Munro and Freud thereby each creating a (metafictional) world whose exposition incarnates a constitutive truth about the formation of the subject.

The dizzyingly recursive fictions through which subjectivity is produced are one reason, Butler (2005) argues, that the self can never be reducible to narrative competence. When we try, like Janet, to give an account of ourselves, our narrative, she suggests, 'begins in *media res*, when many things have already taken place to make me and my story possible in language. I am always recuperating, reconstructing, and I am left to fictionalize and fabulate origins I cannot know' (p. 37). Just as the *mise en abyme* of the planetarium scene in Munro's tale offers an endless self-mirroring that blurs any putative distinction between fiction and reality, between model and what we can know of the real, so too we might say there is a 'blur' at the heart of the subject: no single, distinct version or 'ur-text' of the self but rather a variety of endlessly multiplying forms or narratives in all their 'innumerable repetitions, innumerable variations'. It is this never-ending deferral of meaning that destabilises any foundational account of the self, opening up to us the 'familiar artifice' of a subject whose narrative reconstruction is constantly undergoing revision. Indeed, Munro goes further by insisting we doubt the authenticity of any story we may come to tell about ourselves. For if my origin lies only in that which I have fictioned, how can I affirm its truth? And insofar as my story is 'dazzling, apt and striking', can it ever be anything more than 'an evasion'? How, and by what means, is it possible to have any kind of authoritative knowledge about the self?

Conclusion

Authoritative knowledge, of course, tends to be knowledge whose reference point lies 'out there' in the external world. Rooted in the everyday world of 'morals and manners' (Martineau, 1838), we might, if with some over-simplification, regard the novel as anchored in an external reference point that acts to bind the form, providing a basis for its moral and aesthetic integrity. The referential basis for the short story, however, is somewhat different. While the pith and brevity of Munro's tale do not preclude reference to the external world, the story's 'self-consciousness and stylized arrangement'

(McIntyre 2009, p. 74), its highly choreographed use of flashback and above all its metafictional treatment of writing and representation signal a refusal of contextual details and explanatory logic that would otherwise embed it within the solidarity of the social world. In what then is the short story anchored? Where is the source of its integrity? For the *mise en abyme* at the heart of Munro's tale is not merely a clever post-modern literary device to demonstrate the self's endless refractions of itself; rather, it contains folded within itself an implicit question about what makes for integrity when the very foundation of the subject cannot be guaranteed. How can the self – that which represents most nearly 'who I am' – be sustained in the short story's disjointed and fragmentary way of telling? Recall that *The Moons of Jupiter* comprises eleven stories overall, each one offering an example or *paradeigma* of women's lives. But examples, as Keenan argues, are largely a matter of identification and substitution; and so by offering the reader a series of examples to identify with, we could say Munro's final tale mimes how subjectivity is produced in the place where previously there was nothing but the event of a comparison. Indeed, her extraordinary title story is one that most clearly stands out as resplendent exemplar of the self. Glittering against the cosmic backdrop of ten other fictive lives, *The Moons of Jupiter* dramatises how subjectivity emerges, as it does in Aesop's raven, by way of response to an alterity that always precedes it. In this way, the integrity of the self, like the integrity of the short story, can be thought of as sustained and authorised only by the fabulous artifice of its own origins.

What might this mean for us as psychoanalytic practitioners? In taking the short story as literary model for the subject, it seems we are faced with the responsibility of hearing an account of a life for which no other may be taken as a reference or model. We are exposed to the self's irreducible singularity in which no external frame of reference can be invoked by way of response. In our attempt to establish general laws, lessons or rules that confer on a particular 'case' what Freud (1895) liked to call 'the serious stamp of science' we are apt to be misled by our use of limiting terms and definitions: 'questionable tricks' as Munro might say, that offer false comfort and reassurance in the face of the unknown. Indeed, just as a full view of all the moons of Jupiter is forever unavailable to us, so too our perspective on other people can only ever be fragmented and partial. 'I ask my mind a question', says Janet's father, 'but I can't see all the connections my mind's making to get it' (p. 225). In seeking, like Janet's father, to 'see all the connections' within the inner world of the mind as well as in the external world of the cosmos, we reach out towards yet inevitably fall short of establishing the whole truth.

So we might consider to what extent Munro's 'way of telling' in the short story could be said to shine a light on the kind of insight that psychoanalytic work aims to foster. After all, in contemporary psychoanalysis, the analyst, unlike the author who takes responsibility for creating the short story from his or her own imagination, comes to play an extremely important role in co-constructing stories with the patient, a joint hermeneutic enterprise intended to persuade us of the meaning of a life (Mulligan, 2017). Indeed, current analytic preoccupations with issues of intersubjectivity (e.g. Benjamin, 1990; Ogden, 1994, 2004) mean we are familiar with the idea that such self-narratives partially come to form the patient's constitutive identifications not via any process of imposed narrative authority, but rather via shifting interpersonal dynamics that sponsor, for example, moments of longed-for mutual recognition (Benjamin, 2004). Reading the penultimate, titular scene where Janet and her father work together to remember the names and stories associated with the moons of Jupiter, we are aware that this mutual effort, so close to the narrative work of analyst and patient, constitutes a final, implicit endeavour on the part of both to make meaningful emotional contact: a shared, fleeting attempt that is all the more powerful and touching for its brevity, restraint and indirection. Janet and her father's explanatory fictions here not only generate a comforting narrative that brings them together before their final parting at the hospital; it strikingly indexes the way in which language can paradoxically be a source of both recognition *and* misrecognition: how it can be used simultaneously to convey as well as to camouflage emotion.[2]

So for all its 'dazzling' or untrustworthy nature, and despite the way it constantly 'turn[s] out to be a questionable trick', Munro wants to remind us that we cannot dispense with fiction. Like Winnicott's capacity for illusion, it is crucial to, and indeed constitutes, our sense of reality. For in the 'phony temple' of the fictioning self, it seems there is no objective, universal truth to which we can turn. All we have is the 'moment that's explosive', the vivid 'flash of fireflies' that constitutes a condensed, discrete *moment of truth*. '[A]ny life', says Borges (1968), 'no matter how long or complex it may be, is made up essentially of a single moment' (p. 83). The short story's way of telling is one that reveals to us that it is only the integrity of the moment itself - 'the fleeting, emerging and vanishing mental content' (Cassirer, 1946, p. 18) - that can ultimately assume exemplary or representative status within a life. It is a moment to which we might well attend. For in the patient's own 'work with words' - within the telling of a dream, the temporary forgetfulness, the careless slip of the tongue - we may find, along with Munro and Freud, where the foundational fiction of the self, the subject, most unavoidably lies.

Notes

1 All references in the text to *The Moons of Jupiter* are taken from Munro, A. (2007). *The Moons of Jupiter*. London: Vintage Books.
2 Whilst Munro's moral struggle with language seems to focus mainly on its insufficiency in adequately representing reality, Winnicott (1963) might take a very different perspective, arguing that language risks exposing too much. 'At the centre of each person is an incommunicado element' he writes, 'and this is sacred and most worthy of preservation. [...] traumatic experiences that lead to the organization of primitive defences belong to the threat to the isolated core, the threat of its being found, altered, communicated with [...] Rape, and being eaten by

cannibals, these are mere bagatelles as compared with the violation of the self's core' (p. 187). Earlier in the story, Munro does not tell us why Janet's adult daughter wishes to 'remain incommunicado for a while' (p. 221), but we learn that in the past, Janet had needed to withdraw emotionally when Nichola was a toddler and at risk of a diagnosis of leukaemia: 'I worried that she would feel the wind between the cracks of the manufactured holidays, the manufactured normal days' (p. 230). The connection between these events and Nichola's subsequent refusal to communicate with Janet in adulthood is unarticulated by Munro though it might be thought to imply that conversation between them risks exposing something traumatic in their relationship. Munro's concern with 'dramatizing what ought to be a most secret activity' (p. 217) thus seems to point to the potential for a double danger associated with the use of language: that it can be both too distant from reality as well as too revealing. The naming of the moons could be seen as pointing to a similar anxiety on the part of Janet and her father that speaking directly to each other about their relationship might be felt as too exposing.

References

Ambuel, D. (2007). *Image and Paradigm in Plato's Sophist*. Las Vegas, Zurich, Athens: Parmenides Publishing.
Bakhtin, M. (1981). *The Dialogic Imagination. Four Essays by Michael Bakhtin*, ed. M. Holquist. Austin, TX: University of Texas Press.
Baxter, C. (2008). *Burning Down the House: Essays on Fiction*. Minneapolis, MN: Graywolf Press.
Benjamin, J. (1990). An outline of intersubjectivity: the development of recognition. *Psychoanalytic Psychology*, 7S: 33–46.
Benjamin, J. (2004). Beyond doer and done to. An intersubjective view of thirdness. *Psychoanalytic Quarterly*, LXXIII, 1: 5–46.
Borch-Jacobsen, M. (1993). *The Emotional Tie. Psychoanalysis, Mimesis, and Affect*. Stanford, CA: Stanford University Press. Borges, J. (1968). *The Aleph and Other Stories: 1933–69*, trans. Norma Thomas di Giovanni. New York: E. P. Dutton.
Brooks, P. (1984). *Reading for the Plot. Design and Intention in Narrative*. New York: Alfred A. Knopf.
Butler, J. (2005). *Giving an Account of Oneself*. New York: Fordham University Press.
Carrington, de Parr, I. (1989). *Controlling the Uncontrollable. The Fiction of Munro*. DeKalb: Northern Illinois UP.
Cassirer, E. (1946). *Language and Myth*, trans. Suzanne K. Langer. New York: Dover Publications Inc., 1953.
Cavarero, A. (2000). *Relating Narratives. Storyelling and Selfhood*, trans. Paul Kottman. London: Routledge.
Derrida, J. (1975). The purveyor of truth. *Yale French Studies*, No. 52 (Graphesis: Perspectives in Literature and Philosophy): 31–113.
Eliot, G. (1876). *Daniel Deronda*. London: Penguin Classics, 1995.
Felman, S. (1977). To open the question. *Yale French Studies*, No. 55/56: 94–207.
Forster, E.M. (1927). *Aspects of the Novel*, ed. Oliver Stallybrass. London: Penguin Books, 2005.
Freud, S. and Breuer, J. (1895). *Studies in Hysteria*. London: Penguin Classics, 2004.

Freud, S. (1912–13). Totem and Taboo. In: J. Strachey (ed. and trans.), *The Standard Edition of the Complete Psychological Works of Sigmund Freud*, Vol. 13, pp. vii–162. London: Hogarth.
Freud, S. (1917). Mourning and melancholia. In: J. Strachey (ed. and trans.), *The Standard Edition of the Complete Psychological Works of Sigmund Freud*, Vol. 14, pp. 237–258. London: Hogarth.
Freud, S. (1921). Group psychology and the analysis of the ego. In: J. Strachey (ed. and trans.), *The Standard Edition of the Complete Psychological Works of Sigmund Freud*, Vol. 18, pp. 65–144. London: Hogarth. Gelley, A. (1995). *Unruly Examples: On the Rhetoric of Exemplarity*. Stanford, CA: Stanford University Press.
Gordimer, N. (1976). The flash of fireflies. In: Charles May (ed.), *Short Story Theories*, pp. 178–181.
Heble, A. (1994). *The Tumble of Reason: Alice Munro's Discourse of Absence*. Toronto: University of Toronto Press.
Holmes, J. (1993). Attachment theory: a biological basis for psychiatry? *British Journal of Psychiatry*, 163, 4: 430–438.
Howells, C.A. (1998). *Alice Munro*. Manchester: Manchester University Press.
Jameson, F. (1989). *The Political Unconscious. Narrative as a Socially Symbolic Act*. London: Routledge.
Keenan, T. (1997). *Fables of Responsibility*. Stanford, CA: Stanford University Press.
Kirova, M. (1997). Psychoanalysis and literature: reading the third text. *The European Legacy: Toward New Paradigms*, 2, 3: 462–467.
Lacan, J. (1959–60a). *The Seminar of Jacques Lacan, Book VII: The Ethics of Psychoanalysis*, ed. Jacques Alain Miller, trans. Dennis Porter. New York: Norton, 1986.
Lacan, J. (1959–60b). *The Seminar of Jacques Lacan, Book XVII: The Other Side of Psychoanalysis*, trans. Russell Grigg. New York: Norton, 2008.
Lacoue-Labarthe, P. (1990). *Heidegger, Art and Politics*, trans. Chris Turner. Oxford: Blackwell.
Leitch, T. (1989). The debunking rhythm of the American short story. In: S. Lohafer and J. Clarey (eds), *Short Story Theory at a Crossroads*. pp. 130–147. Baton Rouge: Louisiana State University Press.
Lounsberry, B., Lohafer, S., Rohrberger, M., Pett, S. and Fedderson, R. (eds) (1998). *The Tales we Tell: Perspectives on the Short Story*. Westport, CT and London: Greenwood Press.
Lukacs, G. (1916/1971). *The Theory of the Novel*, trans. Anna Bostock. Cambridge, MA: The MIT Press.
Martineau, H. (1838). *How to Observe Morals and Manners*. London: Routledge, 1989.
May, C. (1984). The nature of knowledge in short fiction. *Studies in Short Fiction*, 21: 327–328.
May, C. (1996). Prolegomenon to a study of the short story. *Studies in Short Fiction*, 33, 4: 461–473.
May, C. (2012). The short story's way of meaning: Alice Munro's 'Passion'. *Narrative*, 20, 2: 172–182.
May, C. (2013). *The Short Story: The Reality of Artifice*. New York: Routledge.
Mayberry, K. (2009)."Every Last Thing . . . Everlasting": Alice Munro and the Limits of Narrative. In *Bloom's Modern Critical Views: Alice Munro*. New York: Infobase Publishing.
Mazzoni, G. (2017). *Theory of the Novel*, trans. Zakiya Hanafi. Cambridge, MA: Harvard University Press.

McIntyre, T. (2009). The way the stars really do come out at night. The trick of representation in Alice Munro's 'The Moons of Jupiter'. *Canadian Literature*, 201: 73–88.
McKeon, M. (2000). *The Theory of the Novel. A Historical Approach*. Baltimore: The Johns Hopkins University Press.
Milner, J-C. (2016). The tell-tale constellations. S. *The Journal for the Circle of Lacanian Ideology Critique*, 9: 31–38.
Mulligan, D. (2017). The storied analyst: desire and persuasion in the clinical vignette. *The Psychoanalytic Quarterly*, 86, 4: 811–833.
Munro, A. (1972). The colonel's hash resettled. In: John Metcalfe (ed.), *The Narrative Voice*. Toronto: McGraw-Hill Ryerson, p. 182.
Munro, A. (1983). *The Moons of Jupiter*. London: Vintage Books, 2007.
Natali, C. (1989). The problems of human acting and the use of examples in some Greek authors of the 4th Century B.C. *Rhetoric Society Quarterly*, 19, 2: 141–152.
O'Connor, F. (1963). *The Lonely Voice: A Study of the Short Story*. Cleveland: World.
Ogden, T. (1994). The analytic third: working with intersubjective clinical facts. *International Journal of Psycho-Analysis*, 75: 3–19.
Ogden, T. (2004). The analytic third: implications for psychoanalytic theory and technique. *Psychoanalytic Quarterly*, 73: 167–195.
Patea, V. (2012). *Short Story Theories. A Twenty-First-Century Perspective*. Leiden, Netherlands: Brill.
Poe, E.A. (1842). Hawthorne's Twice-Told Tales. Found at: https://resources.saylor.org/wwwresources/archived/site/wp-content/uploads/2011/11/SAYLOR-ENGL405-3.1-TWICETOLDTALES.pdf.
Rader, R. (1993). The emergence of the novel in England. Genre in history vs history of genre. *Narrative*, 1, 1: 69–83.
Redekop, M. (1992). *Mothers and Other Clowns*. London: Routledge.
Rizq, R. (2018). The Figure in the Carpet: Psychoanalysis and ways of reading. *American Imago*, 75, 4: 517–542.
Roberts, G. (2000). Narrative and severe mental illness. What place do stories have in an evidence-based world? *Advances in Psychiatric Treatment*, 6, 6: 432–441.
Rohrberger, M. (2004). Origins, development, substance and design of the short story. How I got hooked on the short story and where it led me. In: P. Winther, J. Lothe and H. Skei (eds), *The Art of Brevity. Excursions in Short Story Theory and Analysis*. Columbia: University of South Carolina Press.
Rothstein, M. (1986). Canada's Alice Munro finds excitement in short story form. *New York Times Archives*, November 10, 17.
Schafer, R. (1980). Narration in the psychoanalytic dialogue. *Critical Inquiry*, 7, 1: 29–53.
Seligman, S. (2018). Illusion as a basic psychic principle: Winnicott, Freud, Oedipus, and Trump. *Journal of the American Psychoanalytic Association*, 66: 263–288.
Smith, M. (1915). The fable and kindred forms. *The Journal of English and Germanic Philology*, 14, 4: 519–529.
Steedman, C. (1992). *Past Tenses*. London: Rivers Oram.
Strachey, J. (1955). Editor's note to Freud, S. (1912–13). Totem and Taboo, some points of agreement between the mental lives of savages and neurotics. In: J. Strachey (ed. and trans.), *The Standard Edition of the Complete Psychological Works of Sigmund Freud*, Vol. 13, pp. vii–162. London: Hogarth.

Trussler, M. (1996). Suspended narratives: the short story and temporality. *Studies in Short Fiction*, 33, 4: 557–577.
Voltaire (1747). Zadig. The mystery of fate: an oriental tale. In: *Zadig and Other Tales*. London: Forgotten Books, 2017.
Walsh, J. (2017). On the seductions of psychoanalytic story-telling: Narcissism and the problems of narrative. *Frontiers of Narrative Studies*, 3, 1: 71–88.
Winnicott, D. W. (1963). Communicating and not communicating leading to a study of certain opposites. In: *The Maturational Processes and the Facilitating Environment*. London: Hogarth Press, 1965, pp. 179–192.
Woolf, V. (1929). Phases of fiction. In: *Granite and Rainbow*. London: Hogarth Press, 1958, pp. 93–146.

Index

abductive reasoning 86–87
Abraham and Torok 100–101
afterwardsness *see* Nachträglichkeit
anagnorisis 77–78, 80, 87
anatheism 44, 47
Apter, E. 29–30, 31, 32
Attridge, D. 5
Auerbach, E. 45

Barnes, J. 12
Benjamin, J. 127
Benjamin, W. 31–32
Borch-Jacobsen, M. 122–3
Brooks, P. 6, 7, 111
Butler, J. 18, 52, 125

case history: vs academic report 82, 84–85, subject of 87–89; *see also* literary genres
Cassirer, E. 118, 127
cataleptic knowledge 79–82; 84, 87
Cave, T. 77–78, 85–86
clone: in literature 22; imitation 28; uniqueness, 29; ontological status of; textual 32; human kinship with 35
Connolly, C. 30
Controversial Discussions 67–68
creative reading *see* literature
cultural message 66–67
Barnes, J. 12

De Bolla, P. 12, 18
Derrida, J. 48–49, 111
Dueck, A. and Parsons, T. 106

Eigen, M. 50
enigma 60, 65, 65–67, 69–70, 72

enigmatic signifier 64 *see also* Nachträglichkeit
eucharistic: as aesthetic 107–108; hospitality 105; imagery of 93; meal 102
Eysenck, H. 6

fable 119–121, 122, 125
faith: in psychoanalysis 40–41, 49–51; in fiction 46; vs belief and knowledge 47; in art 48–49
Felman, S. 6, 18, 52, 111, 113
Felski, R. 8, 18
Ferenczi, S: Confusion of the Tongues, 14–17
Forrester, J. 89
Fra Angelico 38–39, 47, 53
Freud, S: Creative Writers and Daydreaming 5; Elisabeth von R 111, 122; and Ferenczi 14–15; Fragment of an Analysis of a Case of Hysteria 88; Future of an Illusion 40; Katharina 88; literary vs scientific knowledge 81–82; Mourning and Melancholia, 100, 123; Project for a Scientific Psychology 3; on psychoanalysis and literature 3–4, 5–6; on psychoanalytic case history 87–89; and religion, 40; and resistance 1–2; Studies in Hysteria 81, 121–122; 82; Totem and Taboo 121–122; on unconscious knowledge 86; Wolf Man 30
Frosh, S. 8
Frost, R. 18
Fuss, D. 22

Ghent, E. 41, 50–51, 53n2
Gordimer, N. 118

Greenberg, J. and Mitchell, S. 57
Grosz, S. 36

Hardy, B. 57
Heaney, S. 17
Hodge, B. 38–39
Holmes, J. 111
hospitality 48–49, 99, 105

identification: as basis of subjectivity 100; as constitutive of the ego 32, 100, 121, 122–123; in formation of the self 22; defensive 15; in faith 100; in false self 28; founding father 122–124; metaphorical 101–102; in reading 121; in relation to the Other 108n2
incorporation 100–101

Joyce, J. 89

Kazin, A. 5
Kearney, R. 39, 44, 46–47, 94, 108
Keenan, T. 121
Kermode, F. 28
knowledge: academic vs experiential 3–5; 75–76; in faith 47–51; general vs specific 85, 89–90; Jamesian quest for 62; literary, 3–5, 8,16, 65; in novel vs. short story 125–127; oedipal 77; psychoanalytic 7, 16, 18–19; as realization 83, 89; representation of 116; resistance to 1–2; 14, 16; of suffering 78–79
Kristeva, J. 101–102, 105–106, 108n2

Lacoue-Labarthe, P. 123
Lacan, J. 101, 108n2. 122, 123
Laplanche, J. 30–31, 58, 64–67, 70
Levinas, E. 48, 99, 106, 108n2
Levy, L. 57
literature: creative reading 57, 67; and literary criticism 63, 67, 71; relationship with psychoanalysis 5–7, 18–19, 111; and psychoanalytic 6, 58, 68–69
literary genres: case study vs scientific report 82; vs short story 89–90, 110–112

Marcus, S. 88
May, C. 113, 118
Miller, J. 61

Modell, A. 31
mourning 72, 100–101, 105, 114
Mulligan, D. 89
Murdoch, I. 90

Nachträglichkeit 30–31
narrative: autobiographical, 124; and coherence, 89, 110–111; competence, 125; form 82, 94; in Greek tragedy, 46; mythical, 117; sacred 45; of origins, 26; in psychoanalysis, 87–89
Nussbaum, M. 79, 82–84, 89

Ogden B and Ogden, T, 8
O'Grady, K. 101–102

Paz, O. 29
Peirce, C. 86
Phillips, A. 6

Rashkin, E. 101
Ricoeur, P. 94
Rieff, P. 40
Rimmon, S. 57
Rivkin, J. 56
Robbe-Grillet, A. 102
Roberts, G. 111
Rorty, R. 33
Roustang, F. 68

sacramental imagination 93–94; 101; 108
Sacks, O. 35
Sedgwick, E. 6
Schafer, R. 111
St. Augustine 105
Steedman, C. 111
Stein, G. 15
Steiner, G. 48–49
stranger: 48, 99, 101–102; 107; *see also* hospitality; Levinas

testimony 44–45, 52
theory: of enigmatic signifier 64–65; of interpretation 16; literary 82, 110 ; psychoanalytic 2, 67–68, 86; 70, 100; of reading 121; of seduction 15
Todorov, T. and Weinstein A. 62
translation 29–32, 34
transubstantiation 93–94, 102–105
Treanor, B. 47

truth: telling the 12, 16; status of in case study 30; sacred 39; in language 45, 117; bearing witness to 52; personal vs general 90; of fiction 120–121; in formation of subject 125;

Virgin Mary: in Annunciation 38–39; bearing witness 52; as story 46; as subject 44
virus of suggestion 63–64, 69

wager: epistemological vs existential 47–48; psychoanalytic 50, 52

Walsh, D. 82, 83
Walsh, J. 111
Warner, M. 39
way of telling 113, 118, 126–127
Winnicott, C. 56
Winnicott, D: capacity to be alone, 71; creative reading 69; and Henry James, 56–57; theoretical language 68–69; transitional space 50–51; 71, 72; true and false self 28; The Use of an Object 50–51
Wood, M. 4–5, 18
Wordsworth, W. 8–10, 13, 14

For Product Safety Concerns and Information please contact our EU
representative GPSR@taylorandfrancis.com
Taylor & Francis Verlag GmbH, Kaufingerstraße 24, 80331 München, Germany

www.ingramcontent.com/pod-product-compliance
Lightning Source LLC
Chambersburg PA
CBHW051615230426
43668CB00013B/2116